AI

M000073387

A must-read. Storytelling is critical for making better sense of complex matters and can help, in particular, to come up with a clear strategic vision.

Prof. Dr. Peter Lorange, former President of International Institute for Management Development (IMD) and author, *The Business School of the Future*

Read this lively, lucid and persuasive book to learn why a telling story is a far more powerful way to persuade people than a power point. Not surprisingly, its author is connected with magical India, one of the world's greatest story telling cultures.

Gurcharan Das, author and former CEO of Procter & Gamble, India

This book is a gem. The writer's use of his personal stories to teach what he preaches makes it highly readable; it evokes empathy and leaves the reader with precious ideas which click and stick. The many practical tips and hacks bring the art of story telling within reach of anyone, even outside of the targeted business audience.

Janet Lim, Advisory Board member at the Institute for Societal Leadership and Fellow of the School of Social Sciences at Singapore Management University Former Assistant High Commissioner, UNHCR

In this definitive guide, storytelling expert Jyoti Guptara draws on insights from neuroscience to demonstrate the fastest way to communicate better.

Publishers Weekly

Tackles a trendy new subject with experience and intelligence, and the writing is powerful, concise and inspiring. I suspect this book will do really well because I think there is a real need. It can help everyone from CEOs in business and non-profits dealing with strategy, to individual contributors.

This book nails it. In a world emptied by division as well as relational loneliness but overflowing with data and noise, great storytelling is often the missing link that keeps us disconnected from meaning, mission, strategy and stakeholder commitment. Guptara inspires us to rethink how authentic storytelling can enhance our influence as formal and informal leaders. It then goes to work showing how to make storytelling into a powerful relationship resource.

Robert E. Hall, author, *This Land of Strangers: The Relationship Crisis That Imperils Home, Work, Politics and Faith*; serial entrepreneur and recovering CEO, USA

Unlocking the secrets to business storytelling will take your business on a tremendous growth journey. Jyoti Guptara guides his reader through the art of crafting and delivering a business's core values and offers through storytelling. With new media dominating the marketplace, Guptara provides practical guidance on how to navigate through the noise. With insights for new and seasoned entrepreneurs, *Business Storytelling for Success* presents the fundamentals for advancement and optimization of your organisation's story, for more personal and business success.

**Jake Fichman, CEO of Goldfish Marketing Inc.
Media Advisor to the Government Press Office, Israel**

As a business leader, I was always aware of the lack of humanity at work, even though we know business runs through relationships. Jyoti's book amazed me with all the practical hints and structures on how to connect and engage with internal, as well as external stakeholders through story-telling. The most exciting part, for me, is on how to develop your personal story. Going through the steps, you as a leader become distinctly humane, which is these days a requirement for people to relate and connect. In your quest to be an authentic leader and truly influence others, story-telling will ease the challenge of getting people behind you and your organization. This is a must-read for those business leaders who want to make a difference – communicate your true self through story-telling and let others connect with you on a personal level.

**Flooris van der Walt, author *Attentive Leadership*,
former VP Global HR Business Processes at
LafargeHolcim**

Business circumstances recently forced me to change some contracts - and even let people go. Very difficult things for an altruistic person like me. I was not sure how to explain to these mostly foreign co-workers how the contract changes were going to affect them and why they were necessary. I discussed these challenges with my business storytelling coach, Jyoti Guptara, and he immediately made several specific suggestions, referring me also to particular pages of this book, in order to help me use a storytelling technique to communicate what was necessary. Thanks to Jyoti's input, the otherwise difficult discussions went easier for both sides.

Manuel von Allmen, CEO of Kandahar Shoes

How do you get heard or noticed in an age of information overload and low attention span or engage effectively with your customers and employees? This book answers these questions and more. Jyoti Guptara beautifully blends the art of storytelling within a business context and shows how you can effectively influence your audience by connecting with them at the level of both heart and mind, leading to a lasting impact. The insights, applications and tools provided in this book can help any leader, be it in communicating a strategic vision, in promoting your products or in creating a positive engagement within your team.

Suresh Theodore, Head, Global Sales, ABB Power Grids

Business leaders have been expected to take responsibility primarily for making profit within the existing framework of law and social custom. By contrast, politicians should seek the overall welfare of everyone in the community. Where politicians fail in that high calling, could it be because of the stories they tell themselves and others? I believe so because Jyoti Guptara's essential work has helped me to reflect further on that. Telling stories is our best means of sharing hope and communicating so that enthusiasm, energy and love can shine through. Whether you are a political, social or business leader, this punchy, precise and incisive book will help you to exercise a new height and a vastly extended reach of influence and impact.

Dr. h.c. Nik Gugger, Member of Swiss Parliament, social entrepreneur and former Supervisory Board member of Zürcher Kantonalbank

Jyoti Guptara is uniquely positioned to provide a solid business consultancy and strong story-based vision. He shows a remarkable ability to combine creative writing and story-telling with the requirements of executive-level success. Superb writing … The concepts are broken down into clear elements that can be easily absorbed and applied.

Davis Bunn, mega-bestselling author, former international business consultant, Writer in Residence, Regent's Park College, University of Oxford, UK

Find out how a compelling story will drive your business, and help change the world. Guptara's compelling book gives the simple steps we all need to take to open people's eyes, touch their hearts, and move them to action.

Patrick Dixon, Chairman of Global Change Ltd. one of the '20 most influential business thinkers alive'

JYOTI GUPTARA

BUSINESS STORYTELLING
FROM *HYPE* TO **HACK**

BUSINESS
STORYTELLING
FROM *HYPE* TO **HACK**

Unlock the Software of the Mind

Jyoti Guptara

Pippa Rann
books & media

Pippa Rann Books & Media

An imprint of Salt Desert Media Group Ltd.

www.pipparannbooks.com

Short story *Implement* from Significant Objects study
reprinted by permission.

ISBN 978-1-913738-98-3 (paperback)

ISBN 978-1-913738-99-0 (ebook)

ISBN 978-1-913738-97-6 (audiobook)

Subjects: Business | Leadership | Success
Psychology | Communication | Life Hacks

Contents

Premise

From Hype to Hack

W hen you have an important message, you need to communicate it so that it 'clicks' (makes immediate sense) and 'sticks' (is memorable, repeatable, and consistently acted upon).

You can hack this communications challenge with stories.

Storytelling has become a buzzword in business, especially in marketing. There is corresponding scepticism by non-believers as well as disillusionment by people who have either tried and not been satisfied with their own performance, or have tried and not been satisfied with the results.

This book is about taking people beyond the hype. Telling stories is a brain hack. This is your hacker's guide.

In business, we tell stories to get results, not to entertain. Even if the intended result is to build a genuine connection. Yes, stories hack the brain, but what you're really hacking is *what gets in the way* of a human connection. Think of it like shedding unnecessary baggage and cutting to the chase.

Stories are not merely for content creators and marketing departments. Storytelling in a broader sense – giving clarity, meaning and motivation – is something that is relevant to every department in every industry, at every level. It is mission critical.

CEOs don't need to work out all of the organisation's stories, but they do need a working understanding of how stories operate and where they need deploying. They must have what Forbes magazine calls the #1 business skill: *narrative competence*. That's what this guide will do for you.

Too busy to learn yet another skill?

That's why I wrote this booklet. It's the hack to understanding your ultimate communications hack. It will, at the very least, help you to see the incredible potential of business storytelling and why it's worth your time.

In just a few pages each, you can explore the power of storytelling for 7 key areas of life and business, from becoming a more interesting conversationalist to getting buy-in for an idea. Detailed instructions and failsafe methods are beyond our scope, but there are plenty of practical tips.

I won't spell out applications for specific functions and settings such as board meetings, public relations, investor relations, change management, product management, corporate culture, M&A, JVs, and so on. That will require another book. But we must be able to actually tell a good story. That's our final hack. When you can tell a story, you can apply it to whichever function and arena you're in.

Versatile storytelling will *save you time for the rest of your life* as people receive, believe and remember your message. It will also save you money – communication errors are costing your organisation in many ways. Storytelling is a shortcut to rectify a lot of needless mistakes. A hack. It's quick, simple, and free.

That's why I say that storytelling is the *quickest, cheapest and deepest way to more influence*.

Mastering storytelling can make you more successful, but perhaps more importantly, it will help you reconnect your life and business with your humanity and make you happier. It will help you hack yourself.

Don't take my word for it. Start hacking.

Part 1:

Why and How Stories Hack

You can have the best technology, you can have the best business model, but if the storytelling isn't amazing, it won't matter.

- Jeff Bezos, Amazon founder

Jerry Kaplan, 29, started to fidget. He was standing outside the conference room at the most prestigious venture capital firm in Silicon Valley, Kleiner Perkins, and he was about to blow his pitch.

The entrepreneur pitching inside had a crisp colour graph projected on a whiteboard; the man's perspiration gleamed in the reflected blue light. Kaplan had thought this was going to be an informal get-together. Looking at the partners grilling the entrepreneur, Kaplan realised he was utterly unprepared. He had no business plan, no charts, no financial projections, no prototypes. All he had was a maroon leather portfolio holding a pad of blank paper.

What did Kaplan do? He did what every writer does when faced with a blank page. He told a story. The story of a new technology he wanted to develop that would take PCs from clunky boxes to something you would take notes on unobtrusively during a meeting – today's tablet.

After talking for ten minutes nonstop, he could see the partners narrowing their eyes at him. Thinking there was nothing left to lose, Kaplan decided to go all-in with his storytelling approach.

"If I were carrying a portable PC right now, you would sure as hell know it. You probably didn't realize that I am holding a model of the future of computing right here in my hand."

So saying, Kaplan tossed his maroon leather case in the air. It slapped into the centre of the table, shocking the respectable partners.

"Gentlemen, here is a model of the next step in the computer revolution."

For a moment, he thought this final act of drama might get him thrown out. They were sitting in stunned silence, staring at his plain leather folder —which lay motionless on the table— as though it were suddenly going to come to life. One of the partners slowly reached out and touched the portfolio as if it were some sort of talisman. He asked the first question.

"Just how much information could you store in something like this?"

Before Kaplan could respond, one of the other partners did. "It doesn't matter. Memory chips are getting smaller and cheaper each year, and the capacity will probably double for the same size and price annually."

From that point on, Kaplan hardly had to speak. His story had fired their imagination. They didn't care about his missing projections. The partners and associates fleshed out this new business opportunity themselves.

Kaplan had stumbled upon a timeless truth. Good stories are not confrontative; they are collaborative. Instead of grilling him, the venture capitalists were *helping* him. Of course, they didn't see it that way, because it wasn't a pitch. It was a puzzle they wanted to solve.

Kaplan left the meeting feeling relieved, but without high expectations. After all, he'd only sold them a story.

Not much later, Kaplan got a phone call from one of the partners saying they had decided to back him. Kaplan was confused. He still hadn't given them a business plan – nor asked directly for money. But when the deal closed the next morning, the idea was worth $3 million.

Communication 101

P eople don't hear what you say. They hear what you make them think about.

And how you make them feel.

Why do fakes often supplants facts? What makes ideas go viral? In an effort to understand such questions, Chip Heath studied different kinds of information, including urban legends and conspiracy theories. Based on the patterns that emerged, Chip went on to teach a course called 'How to Make Ideas Stick' at Stanford University, where he is a professor of organizational behaviour. Coincidentally, his brother Dan at Duke University had been studying what made great teachers great. One day, they realised they had both spent a decade working on the same question: how to make information understandable, memorable, and effective in changing thought or behaviour. Combining their research resulted in a landmark book, *Made To Stick: Why Some Ideas Survive and Others Die.*

The Heath brothers came up with six factors that determine the 'stickiness' of an idea. To survive and thrive, messages need to be:

- Simple
- Unexpected
- Concrete
- Credible
- Emotional
- Stories

An idea doesn't have to be all six, but these are the factors for 'SUCCESs'.

Now guess what best delivers the first five factors? It's the sixth: Story. A good story is all these factors in one, the perfect airplane for your message. An ideavirus. Or, as some would have it, the perfect Trojan horse.

White Hat Storytelling

Hacking may seem a crass term to use for something that is, at its most beloved, a communication that touches hearts and connects people. While some are legitimately worried about the abuse of storytelling, the people out to manipulate are already armed and using the tools that aid them in their nefarious purposes, and yes, they're busy storytelling. It's too late to stop that.

This is my attempt to help level the playing field so those of us with authentic messages can benefit from more of the attention and credibility all too often given to untrue or damaging narratives. Do you have a quality product or idea, and a genuine desire to serve your audience? Then don't lower your chances of success by ignoring the simple things you can learn in this short book.

Criminals are not the only people who hack. Organisations employ hackers to *protect* them, too. One term for these people is white hat or ethical hackers. Similarly, by helping you master narrative thinking, this booklet should ensure you and your business are **less vulnerable** to the damaging narratives of others, be these intentional or accidental.

Hacking has a negative connotation, associated with manipulation. So do stories, associated with lying. If this is a concern as you read these pages, you need not worry. If you're ethical, your storytelling will be, too. After all, if someone fudges facts and studies, you wouldn't blame the facts. You'd blame the fudger.

Even if you do think of storytelling as a kind of manipulation, think of it as a *good* one. Just as a chiropractor's manipulation aligns the body, stories can align your workforce, organisation, and customers. 'Manipulation' comes from the Latin *manus* (hand) and *manipulus* (handful). You can think of it as meaning 'to take by the hand'. Taking someone by the hand is the best way of leading people anywhere. So don't blame the act of taking someone's hand. It always depends on where you want to take them.

Having looked at storytelling as white hat hacking, why should you want to become a hacker?

Why Do You Need a Communications Hack?

In a major survey, The Economist Intelligence Unit found that communication barriers are leading to a delay or failure to complete projects (44%), low morale (31%), missed performance goals (25%) and even lost sales (18%) — some worth hundreds of thousands of dollars. Doesn't communication just happen – or not – depending on personal communication styles and interpersonal factors? No. Communication styles are learned and can be changed. And given the paramount importance of communication, most of us don't invest nearly enough in improving it.

Communication is how humans work and work together. We are constantly communicating – with co-workers, clients, our devices and ourselves. Through social media, we are communicating with the world. If we can move the needle and improve communications by just a fraction, it will have an outsized effect, like a lever. That's what this guide is about: ways to leverage stories. Why stories? Why not some other form of communication? We'll break that down in the following sections, but basically because stories are both *efficient* and *effective*.

Often telling a story might seem like a waste of time. Isn't it more efficient to just state the information? Yes, it is – but it's not more effective. Similarly, you might choose to take several hours to discuss an issue with someone, which may (or may not) be effective, but is certainly not efficient. For something to be considered a hack, it must be both efficient *and* effective.

Of course, many organisations do take communications seriously and are constantly trying to optimise workflows, touchpoints and communications tools and platforms, which are especially important for remote work. And your organisation may implement the best digital solutions, but do you often neglect to use the ultimate human technology?

Story is Technology

Contrary to 19th century wisdom, it's not just language that separates us from animals – it's story. Dolphins communicate. *Trees* communicate. But only humans tell stories. Why? Because it's who we are, as we will see in Part 1. We *think* in stories. And because we think in stories, we can't help but listen to them. When we come across a story – in private or professional life – it's like music in a world of noise.

The factors that make stories work are what give humans our unique potential. First and foremost, imagination and creativity. Imagination is the ability to see in our minds what does not exist in front of our eyes. Creativity lets us turn that imaginary vision into reality.

Science and technology only work because we can pass on what we've learned, across space and time, so that each generation can build on previous ones. No internet without electricity. No electricity without the wheel.

In books such as *The Storytelling Animal: How Stories Make Us Human* by Jonathan Gottschall, there is copious research about how story sets us humans apart from animals. Even in our dreams, our subconscious is busy ordering events into narratives.

The ability to codify thought in words and images lets us learn from people long dead – and have the same thoughts in our brains they had hundreds of years ago. So story is the ultimate human technology, because without it, we wouldn't be able to communicate in such a way as to build on the creativity of previous generations.

Story is the software of the mind. It lets us do what only humans can do. If tech is ever able to do what has hitherto been unique to us, it will be because we have made it in our image. No wonder Fortune 500 companies have been eager to explore returning to our first and ultimate technology.

Narratives at Amazon

At the world's leading technology-driven company, Amazon, founder Jeff Bezos banned the use of Powerpoint from internal communications in 2004. Executives start meetings with thirty minutes of silence, during which they read carefully written 'narratives'. Narratives are six-page memos with comprehensive, narratively structured text. No bullet points. No images. Bezos and enthusiastic adopters credit the difficult practice of crafting a narrative report with forcing them to think more clearly and express themselves more precisely. Narratives are the basis for all major decisions at the company. Why?

Growing at breakneck speed and expanding into diverse new markets, Amazon had the challenge of keeping people in different silos on the same page about highly technical, emerging industries such as cloud computing. Bezos was concerned about the increasing difficulty of keeping tabs on things. He was dissatisfied with meetings that started with presentations, where the presenter could waffle their way through the topic. He also found it highly inefficient: often the speaker was interrupted at slide 2 to answer a question answered on slide 8.

Bezos, who loves writing, started demanding and distributing narratives instead. When people have carefully read the six pages, everyone knows what they are looking at. Note the irony – removing visuals helped people to see clearly. Remember our thesis that stories hack what gets in the way of a human connection? Let's jump into the science and see how that happens.

The Science of Story: EASY

While you need more than science to become a storyteller, the power of stories is backed up by science. A cursory search will return a plethora of articles and books on the subject, such as *Story Proof: The Science Behind the Startling Power of Story* by Kendall Haven and *The Science of Storytelling* by Will Storr.

To summarise the growing body of neuroscience and research on storytelling: **we have story-shaped**

brains. Information contained within stories slots into our heads without effort, like fitting pieces of a puzzle. The key word here is *effort*. In my own words, the science of storytelling has come to the conclusion that while dry information is hard to process, stories are **EASY** on the ears. Because stories are an *Effortless Appeal* to the *Senses* that releases *Yearning*.

Effortless

If you've had a good career in business, chances are that along the way you had the opportunity to go back to school. And when you did, chances are you sat in that seminar room and shared this very common experience with your peers: you fell asleep.

Why is listening so tiring? It turns out trying to process information costs energy. Thinking literally burns calories (which is why I'm so skinny!). Specifically, what tires us out is *making decisions*. Our capacity for decision-making is finite, which is why at the end of the day we tend to have less patience for even simple decisions and can get irritable when we have to make them. Ever tried to pick a movie after a long day?

When we are presented with information, our brain has to work hard to sift through it all and assign significance. *Is this bit important, and is it more important than this other thing? How does what I'm hearing now relate to what I heard earlier?* These are small decisions, but decisions nonetheless. Information only appeals to a narrow part of the brain, and it's not the part we want to appeal to until we've got to the meat of our message. With shrinking attention spans, designing your message wrong will mean most people never get to the meat, and miss your message entirely.

People spend around one third of their time daydreaming – unless occupied with a story. Why? Because the subconscious is fully involved. Have you ever found yourself nodding off during a presentation, and then the speaker said something that somehow woke you up again? In most cases, you woke up when you started to hear a story. Why is this?

Appeal

Stories energise us. An average PowerPoint presentation replete with numbers and analyses will activate Broca's area and Wernicke's area, two regions of your brain responsible for processing facts. Story touches up to **seven** regions of the brain. Describing an activity might engage the motor cortex, while describing sounds, smell, taste or touch affect the sensory cortex.

While we've always known stories work, today we can measure the spike in cortisol when listeners are paying attention. We know that the feeling of bonding an audience gets when it empathises with a speaker is oxytocin, the same chemical released when lovers get intimate. Turns out one of the things that helps your messages 'click' and 'stick' is a chemical 'kick'.

Senses

So we know that neurotransmitters are involved, and that stories can have a visceral impact. But why is that? Harvard psychologist Dan Gilbert describes the brain as an experience simulator. The ultimate power of Story – the reason no other communication comes close – lies in the fact that at a subconscious level, *we cannot fully differentiate between the real and the imagined.* That's why your pulse races when you watch a thrilling movie. You know you're sitting on the couch with a bowl of popcorn on your belly, but part of you believes you're *actually there*, in that dark alley, being chased by a psychopath. And when you walk through another dark alley afterwards, you're spooked because your brain is expecting to experience more of what it thinks it just went through.

Yearning

Think of your favourite fictional book or movie. How did it make you feel? I ask this question at most of my workshops, and I always hear variations of the same two responses. First, the best books and movies make us feel more *alive*; they awaken a thirst to live life to the fullest. Second, and somehow triggered by this feeling of aliveness: they make us want to be a better person. A more caring, giving, creative, tenacious person.

While the brain is good at processing information, it's a pattern-finding and meaning-making machine. Feed it bare information and it will tire. Feed it stories and it will come alive. Indeed, stories make *us* feel alive. Maybe it's something to do with order and beauty. We tend to find more symmetrical faces beautiful. In the same way, stories have shapes that we recognise as inherently meaningful. The way music makes us feel. When we come across a good story, it is like music in a world of noise.

With their chain of causality, stories appeal to logic. They *make sense*. By painting a picture of the human condition, stories are also *sense-making* . . . they create meaning. Stories tap directly into the motivation centres of our brains – we're addicted to them!

Not all stories are going to make someone's heart swell, of course. They don't need to. The point of our discussion is knowing that stories can do so, and to understand why, so we can use these principles to hack life and business.

Considering their potential effect on people, stories are deceptively innocent. If you start making statements, people can feel threatened. If you start telling a story, they relax. Stories are a *low threshold, deep impact* communication. When people start listening, curiously, they may think they're in for a harmless anecdote (*Effortless*). But depending on the story, by the end, they are wishing to experience or contribute to something bigger than themselves (*Yearning*).

Stories are EASY:

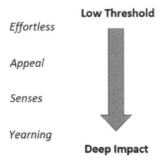

There you have it: an *Effortless Appeal* to the *Senses* that can release *Yearning*. Good stories are easy to hear. Now if only good stories were so easy to tell . . . That's where Part 3 will help you.

There are many different shapes, sizes, and types of stories, from the anecdote to the data story, from the joke to the reality-framing meta-narrative. Even classifying them is beyond our scope. Entire books have been written on these topics. This guide gives you an overview, with the aim of opening up the possibilities of storytelling in areas you may not have thought of including.

Wholistic Hacking

Stories are a hack because they hack *wholistically*. There are various language hacks such as neuro-linguistic programming (NLP) or framing survey questions negatively rather than positively and vice versa. These may fool people for the duration of a survey or event, but don't often have a lasting influence. They are simple psychological tricks. Stories by contrast go deep.

Remember how at a subconscious level we cannot fully differentiate between the real and the imagined? Imagine the implications. If you can tell a story that connects with your audience, they will be where you were. They'll see what you saw, they'll think what you thought, and feel what you felt. You no longer have to tell people things; you can *show* them. And they will likely change their opinion and behaviour based on what they've seen themselves. They will mentally walk in whoever's shoes you want them to walk in and, if you know what you're doing, they cannot help but stumble upon the message you have planted along the way.

The Advantages of Story at a Glance:

Information (Statement)	Imagination (Story)
Explanation	Experience
Inform	Influence
Direct	Indirect
Push (threatening)	Pull (inviting)
Serious – high threshold	Playful - low-threshold
Difficult to process language	Simple language
Costs energy	Releases energy
Removed - cerebral	Immediate - visceral
Abstract	Concrete
Detached from life	Applied in context
Hard to remember	Memorable
No motivation potential in itself	Has the power to motivate
Processed rationally	Processed holistically
Spoon-feeds knowledge	Whets appetite for knowledge
Snapshot of knowledge	Journey of understanding
(Empty?) assertion	Demonstrated proof
Theoretical	Models behaviour

Start Now

Later, I will show you how to start a **story bank**, because having the right stories in your collection is literally as valuable as money in the bank. But please don't wait. You'll want to read this with a pen and paper, as the ideas and stories here spark your own. Make sure to capture those elusive anecdotes.

Jotting down inspiration is much more important than making notes on the theory. The theory you can revisit. When stories emerge from your subconscious, you need to capture them, because they don't often resurface.

If you have pen and paper at the ready, or have created a new file in your notetaking app, then we're ready to explore how storytelling can hack seven areas crucial to personal and business success.

EXERCISE
- What 2-3 things about the science of story excite you? Take a minute to jot down possibilities you think of, in case I don't cover them in the following sections.

Part 2:

Six Areas Stories Hack

No one ever made a decision because of a number.

They need a story.

- Daniel Kahneman,

Nobel Prize–winning economist

1 - Interest

Hack Conversation & Meetings

F rom informal meetings to public speaking: our ability to get ahead stands and falls with our ability to be heard, understood, and believed, personally and professionally. That is the very definition of influence. By engaging imagination and emotion – parts of us that business has traditionally neglected – stories help people receive, believe and remember your message.

Now the intricacies of story can be intimidating. But stories don't have to be elaborate to be powerful. In fact, in business, the simpler the story, the more effective.

I was recently at a Christmas gala in Bern, the capital of Switzerland. Of the seventy invited guests, twenty-two were national ambassadors or their deputies. I got talking with a lady in red, who turned out to be her country's First Consul. We were soon discussing how storytelling could help in her diplomatic work. Eventually she paused and lamented that she didn't have any exciting stories to share. The irony was that she'd just told me how she chose to live in bilingual Biel rather than German-speaking Bern because she struggled to integrate her children into school. This, I pointed out, was a perfect story for connecting with individuals or giving public speeches.

A lot of my clients – powerful people in positions of authority – are worried about boring their listeners, when **everyday** examples are precisely what people can relate to. Hearing about an ambassador's difficulty with her children's education humanizes her, the otherwise remote holder of a high diplomatic office. Incidentally, the Christmas gala conversation above is an example of a simple story. It takes under a minute to recount and has a clear point: stories don't have to be exciting to be effective.

Do you have a list of short stories like this to explain what you do, answer frequently asked questions and counter common objections? You should. Chances are, if you give storified answers, you won't have to answer the usual objections. Two or three stories might be convincing enough you can skip the others.

Don't try to pack more than one point into each story. As in the case of a laser, **focus** is what gives power. I'll give you much more on how to spot, collect, and practice telling stories later. For now, just know that as long as listeners can see how the story relates to the topic, the more we leave out, the more clearly the point is made. As the author of *Le Petit Prince,* Antoine de Saint-Exupery once said: "Perfection is not when there is no more to add, but no more to take away."

If there's anywhere there's plenty to be left out, it's in the area a creative writer learns to cut most ruthlessly: dialogue.

From Small Talk to Conversational Capital

Let's face it: small talk is boring. And it's often unproductive. By Einstein's definition, we are all insane. He (supposedly) said that insanity is doing the same thing over and over again expecting a different result. We do this in social interactions all the time.

How are you?

"Fine."

What do you do?

"I'm a business consultant."

Yawn. How many times have you caught yourself mentally checking out as you listen to yourself giving the same old answers? Especially when you already know the other person is going to get just as glassy-eyed. When they do, we blame them (they asked us!).

If something doesn't work, shouldn't we switch tactics? But some things are so familiar, we don't even realise they're broken. And isn't that routine merely small talk anyway? Sure . . . But why do we do small talk in the first place?

Let's disrupt small talk!

Instead of killing time, why not treat every interaction as an adventure, an opportunity to mix things up? Every interaction becomes an opportunity, a chance for a sale, a lead, a follow-up. To encourage or challenge someone. To try and learn something about a subject matter you maybe thought you would never care about, and be open for surprises.

But most importantly, that way it's not boring. It's definitely not boring to you, and chances are, also less boring to the person you're talking to. Being interesting makes you memorable, and being memorable is what creates leads. Maybe not with that very person, but they will remember who you are and what you do and when something comes up later, they will say: "Hey I remember a guy who'd be perfect for you!"

Give people what they want, not what they ask. Beware when someone asks, "How are you?" Chances are, they don't want to know. Oh, they want *an* answer all right, but not to the question they asked. What they're really doing is inviting you to share something entertaining or enlightening. They're asking for a *human connection*. So oblige them.

When people dial into the *The Dave Ramsey Show* and ask how he is, he responds, "Better than I deserve." A nice tongue-in-cheek answer. Depending on how much you think about it, you may find it funny, intriguing, or disturbing. But it's different. You could respond with humour: "I'm great, but I'm totally biased." Or: "I'm fine right now, but there's still time for things to go horribly wrong!"

A friend, Christian Busch – author of *The Serendipity Mindset* and a director at NYU's Center for Global Affairs – told me about an entrepreneur in London he knows who uses three conversation hooks. If you tell people you meet that you practice law, support Liverpool Football Club, and are on a mission to create a carbon-free economy, they'll have three quite different options for the kind of conversation they might want to pursue.

All of these responses go further towards giving the human connection. But of course, if the setting permits, the best thing to do is to give them a little story.

This simple habit alone will make you **'an interesting person'** people want to be around – and probably do business with. Why? Because you've repeatedly given them the chance to know more about you than that you're 'fine'!

It's worth making that impression even on people who are not immediately of interest to you or your business because you never know who they know. Try and treat every conversation like you're living in a village where everything you say or do will come back to you eventually.

Every day, opportunities to connect and effectively lead, or to convert leads into sales, are lost – because we don't use the most simple and powerful communication tool. How do you best communicate with a human? You treat them like a human. And because humans are 'the storytelling animal', you tell them a story.

What did you experience recently? It could be something you were struggling with and a realisation you had. Or how someone helped you overcome a challenge (the perfect opportunity to give credit and to be humble at the same time). It could simply be something you are grateful for, and why that thing is meaningful to you.

This way of thinking takes getting used to, but it isn't hard. Just, 1) ask yourself: What do you want people to notice you noticing? 2) Then *actually notice those things*, and 3) tell stories about noticing them.

Remember that notebook I advised carrying along with this book? Start jotting down the small things you notice. They probably won't be complete stories, but they will help you to start noticing what you need to.

This 'enhanced small-talk' is the easiest and most effective way to let people know things about you, day in and day out. An example: If, at this very moment, as I'm writing this, a friend was to ring and ask how I am, I'd tell them I really enjoyed lunch, which I got to eat with my wife because she is working from home during the Covid-19 coronavirus lockdown. We had fried rice. She prepared the veggies, I did the rice. I'd mention that I used to hate chores like washing rice before you boil it . . . but now I actually relish the feel of the rice between my fingers, and it gives me a chance to reflect and be grateful that we always have enough to eat.

My friend can hopefully read a lot from my answer: that I enjoy spending time with my wife … that I help in the kitchen … that I'm grateful … that I try to be mindful, and so on. All these conclusions are fine with me. And hopefully, my friend will think: Ah, this is why I love this guy.

But if a prospective *client* asks me how I am, I'm more likely to mention some work I did yesterday for

ETH Zürich, one of my clients. This person may be impressed to hear about ETH (Einstein's university) and decide I am competent and trustworthy – again, a good conclusion. Ideally, I will want to mention something I learnt on the job. Two reasons: first, I'm not positioning myself as the 'hero' (a role you want to reserve for your customer) and second, you're sharing something of actual interest and not just name dropping. But don't sweat it. Even name dropping is more interesting than 'fine'.

By the way, if you don't have a story of your own, you can always borrow one. Maybe you recently heard or read a story you can repeat. Having simple stories like this up your sleeve is key to building what I call *conversational capital*. You're giving something of value, not piffle. Getting more business in return is the inevitable result. When every interaction can count, you'd better make your words count, too.

On that subject, make sure you're not doing all the talking. Ask questions. Most importantly, fish for stories. If you can get the *other person* to tell a story and you respond with interest, it will make them feel great, and you may get clues about where to go next.

Would you sit next to yourself at a party? Master storytelling, and you would. In Part 3, I will teach you how.

Stories in Meetings

Say we're in the middle of a meeting and we're talking about how to get key information across at an employee event. The marketing manager, Suzie, says: "We need to focus on whittling the information down into soundbites. We can put them into a pretty format and hang them on the walls. People can read them at their leisure over drinks. After all, if we're honest we know no one really cares about the CEO's speech. He already goes on too long. Giving the boss any more information to work in would be a disaster. People just want to celebrate."

This garners some nods. My heart starts beating faster, because I know this won't work. If people are just there to have fun, they're not going to read the artwork either. Even if they do, they won't remember it. Coming up with great-sounding slogans will be a waste of time. I want to make the point: *A good story beats great information.*

Now, because I maintain a story bank (see Hack 7 in Part 3), I have the perfect story to make this point. The problem is: when I tell this story onstage, as a speaker, it takes several minutes. I don't have that kind of time in the meeting. So I summarise the story, making sure I keep the pivotal moment.

I might say something like this: "Great idea, Suzie. The artwork can support our message, but I don't think the information alone will stick with people. I think we need to tell them some stories. I realised how good stories are at making a point the first time I spoke in front of 800 people. I'd prepared this beautiful presentation full of interesting facts, but no one was interested. There was a horrible moment when I was staring out at this sea of faces, and I knew they couldn't care less. Fortunately I remembered that I'd always had a good response when I told stories, so I switched tactics in the middle of the presentation. I told my story, and it saved the day.

People really started listening. More importantly, they remembered. After the event, I got talking with several people, and they all commented on my 'message about perseverance'. Funnily enough, that wasn't really my message. I'd made dozens of points using factual information, but it was only the point I made through the story that struck them and stuck with them. In fact, I saw someone a month after the speech, and they said the same thing. So I feel we should be looking for a gripping story or two that can help people understand why this is important."

"Hm," Suzie might say, "What was your message supposed to be about?"

"That's the thing," I respond. "Looking back, even *I* can't remember."

Amid chuckles, the team starts talking about how we will find stories and who will deliver them. The switch in gears happens quite naturally, and soon the beautiful artwork is forgotten. Even though it's short, the story of how I changed direction back then during my presentation models how we should change direction now in our meeting.

No one is even aware I used a story about how stories beat abstract information to prove the point that stories beat abstract information. Contrast this with what might happen if we disagree with Suzie's suggestion outright. Suzie or the people who agree with her soundbite idea might start defending the art, and we're still talking about art instead of what I think will be better, stories. Not bad for a simple story I can tell in under a minute.

Speak Plainly

The mark of the master is the ability and confidence to put things simply. By contrast, jargon is language people can hide behind. A security shield. Because if we fail, it won't be as much our own personal failing, but that of convention, accepted wisdom, and established ways of doing things. We just did it by the book, and it didn't work.

If on the other hand we dare to bring ourselves into the equation, using our own words or personal story, our whole personality, failure would be much more about us having failed personally.

But that's a thinking error. If you fail, you'll feel bad regardless! Doing it right, following the advice given here, you will win more often using your humanity and personality. And when you do win, success will also be personal. It will be your success and not the success of the numbers or of convention. Not only will you 'win' more often, but you will feel better about every win, because it will be *your* win.

By all means use jargon and abstractions, but do that where it is strictly necessary or most effective, not as your default or out of mere convenience. One of my clients, a senior banker, put it this way: "30 years in banking has given me tunnel vision when it comes to communicating person-to-person. Storytelling helps me overcome that."

Stories force you to speak in plain language, like a human being. Jargon empowers us with a politician's ability to prattle on for minutes without saying anything. Speaking plainly gives people the impression you can think clearly and don't have anything to hide. Which brings us to our next hack: trust.

<u>EXERCISE</u>

- Reflect: Where can I speak more plainly? Where am I trying to distance myself from the work with the excuse of professionalism, and how could bringing my true self to the table lead to more interest – my own and others'?

- Bonus: Look over one of your recent reports or talks or recall a meeting. Where could you have achieved a better result with a story?

2 - Empathy
Hack Trust

B uilding trust doesn't have to take months or years. By employing what researcher Brené Brown calls 'socially appropriate vulnerability', we can quickly connect with people at a level that makes them feel they know us – and hence trust us.

Why do we care about characters in books and movies? Even the bad ones? Simply put: *Because we know them*. We know where they come from, what they want, and why they want it. We've seen them struggle against the odds, and we're cheering them on to success – or willing them to stop before they run into disaster. In the same way, when we tell personal stories well, people start to know and hence care about us. In an age of fake news and AI, the importance of authenticity and perceived trustworthiness will only increase.

Describing the house your grandparents lived in and the misadventures you got up to there may not seem to be directly relevant to your meeting . . . but by establishing or deepening a bond it *is*.

Messenger before Message

Before you can hope for your message to connect, you must, as the *messenger,* first establish connection with an audience. Otherwise you'll be talking to air. No matter the medium, messenger always comes before message. In war, you better see that white flag, or the soldier marching towards you is simply another enemy combatant. If we suspect an email is from a suspect source, we won't open it. And yet it is remarkable how often seasoned business professionals will overlook what is an obvious daily reality: *Before people receive your message, they must first receive you.*

Harvard Business School professor Amy Cuddy and colleagues have been researching first impressions for over a decade. They have identified two questions foremost in people's minds when they first encounter someone. One: 'Can I **trust** this person?' And two: 'Can

I *respect* this person?' Significantly, the study found that even in a business context, trustworthiness was more important than competence. After all, it doesn't matter how educated and intelligent someone is if they're going to steal your money.

Initial trust, that important foot in the door for any new interaction and relationship, is a fundamentally irrational thing. Which makes it the ideal time for storytelling.

If storytelling is one of the differentiators between us and animals, why do we hesitate to use it in business? Perhaps, ironically, it is because of the other thing that makes us human: rationality. Because we think we're a rational species, we try to convince each other in as rational a way as possible, avoiding anecdotes and emotion in an attempt to appear trustworthy. Ironically, this often backfires. Attempting to win trust with arguments is hard work, because trust is a feeling. It is logical, then, that connecting on an emotional level is the better route.

With their pattern of cause and effect, stories do appeal to our rational side too. Stories address us not just as intelligences but as *people*, honouring sentience and sensibility.

My aforementioned senior banker client used to work with Jürg Zeltner, then President of UBS Wealth Management with over two trillion in assets. How did Zeltner get ultra-high-net-worth individuals to trust him with their money? He told them a story. When meeting with the world's richest clients, he told them that he actually comes from the countryside. There, people's trust would only have been secured if you were allowed to sit at their kitchen table. That's where the really important decisions are made. With this little story, Zeltner was able to convince super rich people from other countries such as China to trust him with their assets.

After telling this story to his own clients while on the frontline, Zeltner later used it as a metaphor to explain to his employees that they only really have the trust of customers when they're offered a seat at the kitchen table. The personal story told to sway ultra-high-net-worth individuals was now used to teach other wealth managers, modelling a mind-set. This was the approach that in 2015 got him awarded second place among the ten best global private banking CEOs of the year. Zeltner was my client's favourite boss. His townhall meetings always took place without slides and he always spoke freely. On reflection, my client says, Zeltner was his favourite boss because he was among other things an outstanding storyteller. Stories such as the above can help you be received as a *messenger* – by ultra-high-net-worth individuals and by colleagues – so that your message is also received.

Getting Intimate

When an audience imagines a story, their neurons fire in the same patterns as that of the speaker. The brains of storyteller and audience synchronise. When this happens, you can hear a pin drop. The feeling of bonding an audience gets when it empathises with a speaker is oxytocin, the same chemical released when lovers get intimate. Perhaps that's what prompted Princeton professor of neuroscience Uri Hasson to call this effect **'brain coupling'**.

Several years ago, I read an interview with a young lady who had just won the Miss Switzerland beauty pageant. When asked about her religion, she responded: "Faith is a private matter." *How wise!* many readers must have thought. These same readers probably did not bat an eyelid as Miss Switzerland answered the next question about the intimacies of her sex life. But I was dumbstruck. What this girl thought about the meaning of life or ultimate reality – something she shares in common with every human on the planet – was deemed too private to share. But intimate moments she shared with just one person were deemed socially appropriate fodder.

I don't blame the young Miss Switzerland herself, a mere cog in a larger moneymaking machine. Perhaps this was storytelling, intended to build trust with the public by publicly sharing the kinds of things breathlessly shared between girlfriends. The illustration is intended to remind us that storytelling is more intimate than we might think. It's a precious social bond. Let's respect that.

Unethical storytelling may help you amass a fortune, but you're likely to lose it again, as did the perpetrators of the Wirecard and Theranos scams. Even if you're never found out, you won't really be able to enjoy the fruit of lying lips (see *Destiny: Hack Yourself*). Even animals can sense fear, we have a whole host of body language that give cues beyond the words we are saying.

You might tell a technically perfect story, but a lot of people will still sense wrong motives. While scams are sometimes blamed on clever storytelling, it was not so much the brilliance of their stories that fooled people as simple greed. Trust is the social glue that keeps us one step from savagery. Let's try not to compromise it even in the small things. Ultimately, the story that aims to build trust quickly must emerge from its taproot: **trustworthiness**.

The good news is, you don't have to fake a selfless goal with cheesy storytelling. In fact, if you tell us why you're here – what's in it for you – we might be *more* likely to trust you.

Your Why

Making money and being successful are perfectly natural goals. As long as your gain doesn't mean our loss, we don't mind. But bluntly declaring you want to be successful would be boring, not to mention strange. Why should we care? To come up with an effective '**Why Story**', we need to dig deeper and find a motivation someone else can identify with.

For example, if I had to justify my desire to be a successful novelist, some people might identify with my desire to see my name on book covers and in newspapers, but there's nothing vulnerable or emotional about it. It sounds selfish, and it is. If I dig deeper, maybe I'll realise that I want to be a famous author so I can use my time doing more of what *I* want. Financial freedom is about freedom. But if I dig deeper still, I might discover that the real reason I want financial freedom is because: *I want to be with the people who matter to me, when it matters to them.*

In January 2019, two weeks before her 70th birthday, the doctors told my mother there was nothing more they could do for her. Only ease her pain. When I heard my mother was in a hospice, I wanted to jump on the next plane. But I had a job. And since it sounded like she still had some months left, and our family already had plans to gather for her birthday days later, I decided to wait. The end came as a shock. Two days later, my father texted me to 'come as soon as possible' – and I did. A few hours later, I was at Zürich airport waiting to board my plane for London when my sister texted: *She's gone*. My mother was the person who mattered most to me, and I wasn't able to be with her during her final days, when it mattered most to her.

This idea is promising as a personal 'why' for wanting more flexibility because everyone can relate to making family sacrifices for work. Having given this example, I repeat: vulnerability must be socially appropriate. I was able to write the above, but I don't know if I'm going to use it in a lot of public talks. As harsh as it is, a self-indulgent tear-jerker doesn't do anything to build trust, and it isn't appropriate for business. If you start sobbing every time you give your big reason for business, it may be cutting a little too close to the bone.

Still, discovering the connections behind such an emotional story are useful *for you* as a springboard for discovering more stories that are perhaps more fitting, but equally important to you. You don't have to share every story you come up with. So go deep. (Besides, research shows that talking about painful memories is instrumental in healing them.)

Can you connect your goals to what really matters to you? Why do you want to be successful? Why at *this*? Connect us to what's important to you, and we'll feel for you. Next to the Why Story, there are a few other story types which help people to connect with you as a person and the mission you're on. I list them in Part 3.

To find stories that will help you hack trust, you need to reconnect to what makes *you* human, and trust that in yourself.

Story is Collaboration

When you want someone's trust, it's tempting to try and give them all the information. But talking quickly and information overload will backfire. If you find yourself explaining your company or product, stop. Can you let them experience it instead?

Remember that each of us has only a few words in our 'quota'. So why choose to spend them on telling a story? Why not go for the facts? Many reasons, which we touched in Part 1. But we haven't yet listed perhaps the most important one. When people hear a story, they often respond by *telling* one. Which is excellent for two reasons. First, they are engaged. With you, but equally importantly, with their own experiences and thoughts – which they are connecting with you. Second, when you hear what's on their mind, you'll know the right thing to tell them next to move the conversation forward.

Why not expect the other person simply to bring up that subject, without either of you telling a story? Because that's not the way we're wired. If they hadn't shared that story but had stayed at the level of the abstract, chances are they wouldn't have brought it up at all. But because they're an expression of what's on someone's heart, stories cut to the heart of the matter.

There is another sense in which storytelling is collaboration. Stories hack trust because they are a co-creating process. As I speak, you paint. My words become your pictures. This is why you don't have to describe every detail, a mistake many writers make. As the celebrated editor Sol Stein said, "One plus one equals one-half (1+1=1/2)." What he meant by that is that *one* adjective to describe something can add power, whereas two adjectives don't necessarily mean twice as much power. Often they give you only half as much as the original adjective. For example, if someone is 'harried' as they run their hands through their hair, we don't need to say they're 'worried and harried'.

A famous saying goes that fiction is 'real life with the boring parts left out'. The same goes for true stories. And that's OK ... because we know *it isn't the whole story*. It's a frame – a window to help people see what they need to see.

Story is collaboration. And just like we tend to trust someone more if we've collaborated positively, we trust them more after hearing and sharing a story.

The idea of collaboration is especially important for our next hack: buy-in.

EXERCISE

- Why are you trustworthy? Take a minute to write down your qualities. Don't be humble! What's your superpower? What nice adjectives would someone use about you if they were comparing you to the worst person on earth?

- Now take a few minutes and try and connect each of these abstract words with a specific incident. Anyone can claim to be trustworthy, honest or persistence. When did you *demonstrate* trustworthiness, honesty, perseverance, etc.? Next time you need to convince someone you possess this quality, don't make an empty claim. Tell them the story, and they'll come to the conclusion you have that quality.

3 - Agreement
Hack Buy-In

People aren't rational. But when it comes to our most important communications, we tend to try and convince each other with rational argument. One of my more memorable experiences as a storyteller was attending the UN Forum on Business and Human Rights in Geneva. The *Palais des Nations* is labyrinthine and hard to navigate – a good analogy for the UN itself. One of my meetings was with a member of the committees responsible for inter-agency collaboration. She'd been working at the Palais for over a year, but still struggled to find her way to the Bar Serpentine, the main space for conference attendees.

She described how duplication and overlap between the various organisations made her work challenging. Next to the six principal organs of the UN, there are (currently) 15 specialised organisations such as the IMF and WTO, which in turn collaborate with dozens of other so-called 'Related Organizations' for inter-governmental work. Buzzing around all of this are countless NGOs. Each organisation has its own culture and vocabulary. Even where the same words are used, they are often infused with different meanings… The lady lamented how bureaucracy was frustrating for most of the people involved.

"Is UN speak part of the problem?" I asked.

She rolled her eyes. "It *is* the problem."

"Then don't use it," I said. "At least, don't start there. These people didn't want to become lawyers. They're humanitarian workers. It sounds like they need to reconnect to their purpose."

Rather than dealing in abstracts, I suggested that members of the discourse share some significant stories. Why did they get involved in this work? Why with this particular organisation and not one of the others? What was their proudest moment as a member of this organisation that represents what it stands for? Answering these questions would reinforce ownership.

With concrete moments of success and failure before their eyes, everyone would be reminded of their common goals and less likely to squabble over words and turf. The lady left with shining eyes and purpose in her step.

Hearing each other out – not the arguments, but the heart behind them – can be a workaround for endless hours of abstract debate. Stories are often neglected because they are simple. But that is precisely why they work. The deceptively simple framework of a story lets us combine all sorts of things that often don't go together in business – information and imagination, fact and feeling, causality and a greater cause.

When you communicate, do you want to address the narrow part of people that responds to slogans and statistics? Nothing wrong with that. It can work. But you'll get what you bought – only a narrow slice of your people. If by contrast you can engage the whole person – their head and their heart – you will get so much more. And it will show. Passion unlocks potential. Performance *will* improve.

Three Approaches to Communicating a Message

When we have a message for people, we have three choices. We can give people raw information; we can connect the dots for them; or we can help *them* connect the dots.

1) Give people the dots.

Giving people information is like giving them a bunch of dots and letting them come to their own conclusion. 'Let the facts speak for themselves.' The problem is, they rarely do. When confronted with a slew of information, people don't know what is relevant, important, or how it relates to the rest. They're disoriented. It takes a lot of work to figure things out, and they may come to a different conclusion. This, of course, is wonderful – if you want to hear a perspective that challenges your own. Which we all should, before making big decisions. But if you are championing a message, it's *not* what you want. How people connect the dots depends on a string of invisible, internal factors such as psychological biases. And whether they bother to fully engage with the material in the first place. The obvious weakness of this approach is, you don't know how – or even *if* - they are going to connect them. So what you can do instead is . . .

2) Connect the dots for them.

We can make people's lives easier. We can just give them the message directly. But maybe they will disagree with how you've connected the dots and resist your conclusion. Here, you're battling against the same subconscious biases, but also against simple motivation. They may not like your agenda. They will argue over the dots and try and draw alternative pictures. The second approach, too, falls short. When dealing with resistance, connecting the dots for people is not enough to secure buy-in. The invisible factors are still at play. They will argue over the visible – the dots – but what drives them to do so will be invisible factors. So we have to go deeper. Fortunately, we can . . .

3) Help them connect the dots.

Telling stories is the best way to do this. Stories are not confrontational. Storytelling is about entering the mind of your audience so that *they* connect the dots, according to the pattern *you* want them to see. By engaging the emotions, stories can take out the combativeness and make communication collaborative. This is how stories make your message 'click' – information falls into place in such a way that your intended message is communicated. To get buy-in, involve them in the process of connecting the dots.

Every year, millions of businesses and personal relationships suffer unnecessary conflict and damage because we engage with each other at the level of the dots and fail to connect with each other at the level of the invisible. The invisible is the space between the dots. That's where we'll find the keys to motivation and meaning.

Letting audiences connect the dots means letting them own and fill that invisible space. Have you ever finished a book or movie even though you *knew* it would be a waste of time? If there is just one open story loop – a setup that demands a payoff – we keep listening, reading or watching. Why? Because the brain craves completion.

Note that this works even with otherwise terrible stories. If you were glued to your seat despite knowing this was not worth your time, it was because *you* were wondering what would happen next.

Because good storytelling is always a collaboration, we don't want to be spoon-fed information. The best writers don't spell out what the reader can deduce themselves. In Holllywood, that kind of redundancy is known as 'on-the-nose' writing. Great storytellers let **us** connect the dots. That's one of the key techniques that leads to audience involvement – or employee engagement.

Pixar's Andrew Stanton, of *Toy Story* and *Finding Nemo* fame, calls this approach the 'Unifying Theory of Two Plus Two'. In his TED talk he explains:

> Make the audience put things together. Don't give them four, give them two plus two. The elements you provide and the order you place them in is crucial to whether you succeed or fail at engaging the audience. Editors and screenwriters have known this all along. It's the invisible application that holds our attention to story. I don't mean to make it sound like this is an actual exact science, it's not.

That's what's so special about stories, they're not a widget, they aren't exact. Stories are inevitable, if they're good, but they're not predictable.

True: storytelling is not an exact science. Hacking with stories requires a basic understanding of what a story is, but it also requires experience as a story-teller. Later in this guide I'll show you a risk-free way you can practice telling stories. But there is an element of intentional design. Stanton's key phrase here for us is: *The **elements** you provide and the **order** you place them in is crucial to whether you succeed or fail at engaging the audience.* That's what storytelling – including business storytelling – is all about.

I tout my storytelling services as helping you make your messages 'click', or make sense. In order for something to click, two parts must connect. Yes, as a speaker we want to connect with our audience . . . but, as we have seen, a large part of this happens when the audience is given things to connect themselves.

Don't give them 4. Give them 2+2. Make them work for your message, and as long as you give them the clues with clarity, they'll love you for it.

<u>EXERCISE</u>

1. Write down the core of your message.
2. Break the message down into its components (your 'dots').
3. Can you illustrate your dots with small stories that imply your message without your having to state it explicitly?

To summarise, stories get people to think what you want them to be thinking about, without explicitly telling them to think it.

The principle of 2+2 rather than 4 is what makes the classic story technique *show, don't tell* work. If you tell your audience Jack is sad, you're spoon-feeding them. They quickly bore. If on the other hand you tell them that Jack slumped at his desk, mindlessly scrolling while a tear slid down his cheek, we know he's sad without you're having to tell us. We wonder why. We start asking ourselves questions. We are involved.

Audience engagement is wonderful, but let's drill down further on the idea of involvement. Because that is a hack for buy-in.

Ownership and Lottery Tickets

Letting people come to their own conclusion is powerful because what they earn they own, and what they *own* is *theirs*.

In an economic experiment, people were given a bar of Swiss chocolate or a coffee mug. Being Swiss, I was not surprised to hear no one wanted to trade their chocolate for the mug. Probably the value of the chocolate was higher than that of a tinny mug. But that wasn't the case, because no one who had a mug was willing to trade it for chocolate, either! Both sides considered what they owned to be more valuable. Why? Because it was theirs.

This phenomenon is known as the Endowment Effect and was thoroughly studied by Richard Thaler, winner of the 2017 Nobel Prize in Economics. The very act of owning something increases its perceived value to the owner – even if they've only owned it for a very short walk. The implications for organisations are huge. How can we increase ownership and hence the perceived importance of what people are doing?

In another study, involving renowned psychologist Daniel Kahneman, researchers gave half of a group lottery tickets with assigned numbers, and let the other half write their own number. Just before drawing the winning number, the researchers offered to buy back people's lottery tickets. How much more would they have to pay someone who wrote their own number versus someone who was handed a number randomly? Rationally, there should be no difference between the two groups. If anything, the tickets would be worth *less*, given the chance of writing a duplicate number. But what happened? The researchers found that no matter where they conducted this experiment, the response was the same. People who wrote their own lottery tickets wanted at least five times as much as their colleagues.

The ticket was more 'theirs' than a ticket that had been handed with an assigned number. I guess writing their own numbers increased the feeling of being the master of their own destiny. That's the feeling you're paying for.

Incidentally, that was a study story. Consider how much more likely you are to remember the statistic 'five times more invested' with the story and its imagery of lottery tickets than if you had merely read the statistic: 'people are up to five times more invested in something if they were part of co-creating it'.

In a McKinsey study, *The Inconvenient Truth About Change Management*, Scott Keller and Carolyn Aiken ask why the field of change management hasn't managed to *change* anything about change management and the field continues to see the same low rates of success. Two of their first takeaways are 1) You must create a compelling story and 2) You're better off letting them write their own story.

Riffing off the above-mentioned study, Keller and Aiken mention organisations letting stakeholders 'write their own lottery ticket'. It's an example of how stories can give you meaningful vocabulary for discussion as writing your own lottery ticket becomes a metaphor for co-ownership.

A global consumer goods company brought together their top 300 for three two-day sessions over three months, where they created the story together. IBM wanted to rewrite their century-old values and hosted a three-day online discussion dubbed ValuesJam – with 50,000 employees. The result was considered a great success, with far-reaching consequences, from the way IBM interacted with customers to the eventual creation of supercomputer Watson.

The hierarchy of influence

Let's define *influence* as the ability to change behaviour. Professionally and privately, we would all like to change people's behaviour – our own included.

The mistake we make is to think that all we need to do is address the behaviour we want to change. Which is grabbing the tip of the iceberg and wondering why that little lump of ice doesn't budge.

To change what people *do*, we have to change what they *think*. How do we usually try to change what people think? We give them the facts. We try and convince them of the folly of their position, and the superiority of our own. Which of course rarely works, because it puts them on the defensive. You're effectively telling them they're ignorant or stupid. No one likes to be told that. So using facts isn't enough. After all, everyone feels entitled to their own facts in these post-truth days.

We need to go a layer deeper. What determines whether someone agrees with your facts? It's their *feelings*.

Our brain is wired so that connections from the emotional systems to the cognitive systems are stronger than connections from the cognitive systems to the emotional systems. This is why we tend to decide emotionally first, and try and justify our decision rationally later. University of Southern California neurologist António R. Damásio puts it well: "We are not thinking machines that feel, we are feeling machines that think."

If emotion is faster than thought, by the time we get to thinking about something, our emotions have already set our thoughts down a particular path, making it very hard to spot. Some people hold on to the belief they are more rational than emotional because subconsciously they don't like the *feeling* of not being in control – which would of course prove the point.

But there is another, more foundational layer still. What determines our feelings? Sure, various factors come into play, but all else being equal it is the sum of our experiences. Experiences we have made ourselves – but also vicarious experiences our subconscious has 'experienced' by way of a story. And believe it or not, the rabbit hole doesn't end there. Even our experiences and the stories we hear are coloured and interpreted through the lens of our own overarching stories, or meta-narratives.

This, then, is the hierarchy of influence, from ice tip to foundation:

- Behaviour
- Belief
- Feeling (not fact)
- Experience or experienced story
- Sense-making narratives

Can you see why efforts to 'change behaviour' often fall woefully flat? Usually it's because people are addressing the first level, when they need to be drilling three levels deeper, to stories, or four levels deeper, to narratives.

EXERCISE

- Reflect: What foregone conclusions have you been foisting on people rather than letting them connect the dots and come to their own conclusion? Remember: What is theirs, they own.
- How can you create further ownership by letting your team write their own 'lottery ticket'?

4 – Alignment
Hack Strategy

I f you want to be shocked, ask any co-worker what your organisation's strategy is. You won't have to reach to the bottom of the hierarchy before getting evasive answers. The *MIT Sloan Management Review* ran a 2018 article titled *No One Knows Your Strategy – Not Even Your Top Leaders.* Based on data from an anonymized US tech giant, the article describes a CEO reviewing the annual employee engagement survey and being delighted to see that people are so strategically aligned… or so it would seem. Because, while 97% of top leadership *said* that they understood the company's strategy and aligned their work to it, when questioned in more detail by MIT researchers, a very different reality emerged.

Only one-quarter of the managers surveyed could list three of the company's five strategic priorities. One third of the leaders charged with implementing the company's strategy couldn't list even *one*. Similar findings are made across countries and industries – strategy is notoriously hard to communicate. And even when there is awareness and alignment among the top leadership, this clarity never seems to reach the frontline. That is sad and indeed disastrous because it's the frontline that produces the bottom line.

In *Made to Stick: Why Some Ideas Survive and Others Die*, Chip and Dan Heath warn: "If your company doesn't have stories that convey strategy, that should be a warning flag about your strategy – it may not be sufficiently clear to influence how people act. (Otherwise, you'd have some stories to tell.)"

The Four Steps of Strategy

Is it really worth putting the strategy into story form if the content is going to stay the same? You may say, "Sure, it's a bit dry, but so what if they have to read it three times? Let them read it three times a day! It's an

important document and they're being paid for this."
Repetition, repetition, repetition! goes the traditional
advice. Which is better than not repeating your strategy.
But when the strategy doesn't make sense to employees,
you're literally repeating nonsense.

The great irony is that after putting all that effort
and expense into developing the company's strategy,
little thought is put into a strategy to communicate it.
Maybe a slide deck is sent to the various offices. A well-
meaning HQ might bring in people for an expensive
conference, where the strategy is unveiled. The CEO
may travel to the different branches himself to give the
presentation in person. But the hard truth is that if you
use the same thinking to communicate the strategy as
you did to come up with it, you will fail. Because the
rational process you needed to come up with the strategy
lacks the emotion and imagination you need to connect
with people.

As we've seen, chances are that with traditional
approaches, only a small percentage of the decision
makers in your organisation truly understand the
strategy. Now, what percentage of decision-makers do

you think *need* to buy in to the strategy for it to actually be implemented? Do you have enough? And how do those numbers look when you try to see *every* employee as a decision-maker?

Strategy development is not complete until you also have a strategy for communicating it, which requires the following stages:

1. Strategy development
2. Strategy formulation
3. Strategy articulation
4. Strategy implementation and monitoring

Too many companies go straight from step 1 to step 3 . . . and then wonder why step 4 doesn't happen. If the strategy doesn't connect with employees, it might as well not exist at all. Unless it 'clicks' and is both understandable and sensible it won't 'stick' and be remembered and put into action.

If you're still tempted to skip step 2 (formulating the strategy so it can be communicated well), consider that while Hollywood spends over 100 million on making a blockbuster, they spend another 100 million on marketing it. After investing so much into making your strategic message, why wouldn't you invest in communicating it effectively?

You're now ready for the 'secret formula' of an effective strategy story. A lot of leaders instinctively cover the same ground in a different order. But most people also skip one of the four steps, and the order is what gives it power.

The X Story

Storytelling gurus often criticise businesspeople who say they have a 'story' when in fact they have a statement or string of statements. They're right: to get emotional buy-in, it helps to tell an emotional story. But to be fair, these execs are telling a 'story' in the broader sense of a claim or script they hope the company will enact. More precisely, an **explanation**. That's why I call this kind of story an X story. X as in, x marks the spot. ('Ex' as in 'former' also applies to the first of the four steps.)

To recap, when it comes to sizes of story, there are simple stories, immersive stories and the high-level meta-narratives. An effective strategy story is a meta-narrative – an ordering of events into a big picture. It emerges when many smaller stories are structured and communicated well enough that they can in turn actively influence new stories people tell themselves and others as they go about their work with the meta-narrative in mind.

If they have the meta-narrative in mind.

One of the weaknesses of the meta-narrative is that it can be hard to pin down. Even if it can be captured in words, it may still come across as – well, too meta. Abstract and meaningless to front-line employees. There is a simple solution:

a. break the meta-narrative down into narrative steps

b. illustrate the steps with simple stories

In order to break down a narrative into steps, you must know its structure. What's the best structure for a strategy story? Australian business storyteller Shawn Callahan has a simple and effective four-part framework for communicating a new strategy. I call them the Four Ps.

Part 1, *Past*: "In the past…" (how things were before a certain change happened)

Part 2, *Pivot*: "Then something happened..." (the event(s) that caused the problem or opportunity and explain how the present is different from the past)

Part 3, *Present Priority*: "So now..." (the decision(s) made to counter the problem or take advantage of the opportunity)

Part 4, *Pitfalls and Potential*: "In the future..." (the effects of the change – and what is at stake)

Thinking of your explanation stories as X stories will help you in three ways:

- X marks the spot: it gives the big picture.
- If you think of an x as four parts rather than two lines, each line stands for one of the Ps.
- In algebra, x stands for something. Remember to fill in the other side of the equation with anecdotes. Don't leave your audience pulling a blank.

X marks the spot: it gives the big picture. But after giving the big picture, remember to zoom in and *paint* that picture, or it will remain foggy. Paint the big picture as well as the details well, and buy-in will skyrocket. Get the big picture and the compelling snapshot pictures in their heads, and behaviour will change.

This structure is not just for strategy stories. Given their high-level perspective, X stories are good for any kind of (re)framing. They are useful whenever you need to explain a decision, however simple. One of my clients recently called to catch up on a project. He mentioned he had to let some people go. The first conversation had not gone well. I coached him through the structure of an X story, which he employed the following week. While the conversations were still far from pleasant, this CEO did remark that his employees had been more understanding about the economic pressures that were forcing him to let them go.

Just because the framework is chronological, like most stories, doesn't mean you have to come up with the parts in that order. Starting with your Present Priority will help you decide just how far back you need to go to give the decision context.

Not only is this structure useful for communicating a strategy. It can be very useful for coming up with that strategy in the first place. Does leadership agree on the

Four Ps? If not, how do we get agreement? This is where you can kill two birds with one stone. Getting unity on your four-part strategy story and knowing how to communicate it can both be arrived at with an important story principle known as *show, don't tell*.

Instead of 'telling' us that Jack is sad, 'show' us that Jack doesn't want to turn around, and when Sally pulls him around, she feels the stiffness in his arms and sees his tear-streaked face. It's a subtle trick that makes a huge difference in stories, because it leads to *emotional involvement*. 'Telling' treats the audience as 'dumb' because it assumes people need to be told someone is sad, when they should be able to surmise this from the description and dialogue. Over the last three decades, showing rather than telling has become such an expectation within the publishing industry, most editors will turn down a novel for neglecting this one principle.

Instead of telling people the part-two Pivot that changed the way you do business, show a situation and let people come to their own conclusion. Remember: What is *theirs*, they *own*. If you want broad ownership of the company's strategy and values, don't 'inform' people about the situation/problem/solution, give it to them as a story or sequence of stories. Make them see and feel how the new strategy came to be and why. When did you realise your old strategy was no longer going to work? Why did you have that old strategy in the first place, and did it work at all? If it worked, what happened that made you have to change it? If it didn't, when and how did you realize? Show us, and we'll own the realisation.

Overcoming Resistance: The Pre-Empt Story

When people have something specific against you, or a secret objection to your proposal – some reason to discredit what you're saying – they probably won't come out and say it. But their attitude will form an invisible barrier to you getting through. A pre-empt story proves them wrong, indirectly, so you avoid an open confrontation. When a pre-empt story is well told, it will often result in a palpable change in attitude. People lean back and relax, and actually start listening. Now, with the unspoken objection out of the way, you can make progress.

For this to work, it's important to actually know what people are thinking. This is where being a good researcher and listener comes in.

The example we'll use is one that has been in the headlines a lot in recent years, so much so that as a result, many companies have put policies in place that require immediate reporting. But such policies cannot catch attitudes – or perceived attitudes.

Say you are a male supervisor addressing a female employee, and there is a rumour that you discriminate against women. At first you try to ignore it. You want to show through your words and actions that this is not the case. But the suspicion remains and you realize you need to address the rumour. You need to have a good working relationship. You want that employee to bring her good ideas to you and do her best work, which she will only do if she trusts and respects you. You know you need to address the rumour, but you are worried doing so directly could backfire. So you decide to try and remove the elephant in the room indirectly with a *pre-empt* story.

How? Let's look at some options.

It would fulfil the idea of the pre-empt to tell a story about how you appreciated the capability and tenacity of a female employee you went on to promote. But as you can imagine, *how* you tell this story – the way you set it up, your body language and tone – will be very important in determining whether you come across as authentic or disingenuous. So if you are not sure and have not yet had much practice with intentional storytelling, you may not want to tell that story. You could inadvertently end up reinforcing the idea of your power, and the female employee may think this was a 'token' female promotion. It could also seem odd to point out the tenacity and capability of the woman, thus reinforcing the fear that women need to be particularly capable, more so than men, to be noticed and get ahead. The lady employee might then come away feeling her suspicions about you have been confirmed.

Perhaps talking about how your single mum struggled to get ahead in her job for a much-needed promotion would be the better call.

Or an even less direct approach in which you don't talk about gender at all. You may choose to talk about your experience in a more junior position. Say earlier in your own career you had a boss whose door was always open, and this led to great ideas coming from unexpected quarters. You conclude with, "If you have any ideas you think I should hear – or if you ever need help – my door's always open." This gets the message across that you appreciate ideas no matter the source.

Best of all, you might start by mentioning something this particular employee did well and why you appreciate it. *Then* tell the story behind your open door.

That's the pre-empt: instead of disagreeing outright, or being defensive, prepare an individual or a group for your opinion. As with other forms of communication, nonverbal communication is the larger part of the package. Emotional intelligence and social skills are required in choosing and delivering your stories.

A lot of my clients start out over-emphasising a story by subconsciously altering their voice or body language. In doing that, they draw undue attention to the fact they are now telling a story. That undermines subtlety, which is the source of power of even very simple stories. Practicing in front of an audience can help ensure you come across the way you intend, both in terms of content and delivery. Whether in front of an audience of one, such as a coach, or at a live workshop, feedback is an important part of the process. The thing I like about workshops is that everyone can benefit from one person's mistakes (or strengths).

When employees feel appreciated and when they understand your decisions, you will have their respect and affection. Now they can bear detours. Every good story has a struggle – obstacles that must be overcome. Leaders can acknowledge them as such, and people will rally to contribute. Further, having clarity around a common purpose leads to a new level of camaraderie.

Which leads us to the organisation's strategy.

EXERCISE

- Try your hand at your own x story for your strategy, or to explain some other decision (even a domestic one).

- What unspoken objections do people have about your decision, or about you or your organisation in general? What would it look like to disarm them with a pre-empt story? Collect a story or two for each obstacle and save them in your story bank under the hashtag #pre-empt.

5 – Desire
Hack Sales

According to a 2014 study in the *Journal of Consumer Research*, evoking a sense of nostalgia makes people willing to pay more (which might explain why so many brands use retro designs). My theory is that emotionally reconnecting to the past helps us realise how short life is, and that money isn't as important as experiences – or meaning. If this is true and if, as I say, stories are vehicles of meaning, then the value of a story must be quantifiable.

Increase Perceived Value

In 2009, anthropologists conducted the 'Significant Objects' study by asking writers to buy an item from eBay for $1.25. After inventing a story for the object, it was put back up for sale. The same thrift-store junk that had been purchased for a total of $128, with stories attached, now sold for $3,612.

Let's look at one of the stories, which you can find on www.significantobjects.com. I selected one called *Implement* because the implement in question looks pretty useless. I can't actually tell what it is. Perhaps an old, deformed whisk. Apparently it also stumped the writer, John Wray, who kindly allowed me to reprint the story here:

> "It's certainly — well. It's certainly a something," Lily murmured, upon being introduced to the Object. "But what kind of something is it?"
>
> "This," said Oliver, cradling the Object reverently in his open palms, "Is the something that is going to save our marriage."
>
> Not having been birthed yesterday, Lily had her doubts, but she was willing to be persuaded. She was desperate to be persuaded, in fact. And there was something about the something in Oliver's palms that resisted all her efforts to resist it. Unlike most of the objects in Lily's environs, it seemed to raise more questions than it answered. First of all, what was it?
>
> "What is it?" said Lily.
>
> "I just told you," Oliver said patiently.
>
> The Object expressed no opinion.

"Well, we might as well give it a try," Lily said. "How do we make it do?"

Oliver squinted down at the Object for a while, and then shrugged. "I think we just set it down in the corner," he said finally. "Give it room to do its work."

Lily considered this a moment, then took Oliver's hand, and they deposited the object, gently and circumspectly, in the room's nearest corner. "How long will it take?" Lily wondered.

"Ten and a half days," Oliver said firmly. Lily couldn't help noticing, however, that he avoided looking her in the eye. You'll never persuade me that way, Lily said to herself. The Object chittered and hummed in its corner.

"What a strange thing it is," Lily said. "It reminds me of something."

"Shhh!" Oliver whispered. "Don't talk about it. The less we acknowledge it, the better."

It wasn't until weeks later, when their marriage had long since been saved, that they saw the Object for what it truly was. By then, of course, it didn't make the slightest bit of difference.

What was the effect of this whimsical tale? Original price of 'the implement' without story: 99 cents. Final price with story: $20.50. So you see, stories work even for virtually unidentifiable items. The Significant Objects study really is, well, *significant*. Buyers knew the stories were fictitious, and yet they paid an average of twenty-eight times more! This is great proof for the economic power of stories in general. This all happened on eBay. Imagine the potential when you know who you're trying to reach and where they are to be found, the kind of journey they are on, and how your product fits in.

All kinds of stories might help do this. Stories about what goes into the product and what the outcomes are; stories about the kind of person who uses the product, and by extension who you can become (aspirational identity). Products become merely the means to acting out that story. Props. We are likely to buy organic, herbal, handmade soap (and tell people about it) because of what it says about *us*. 'I know James Bond doesn't exist, but this is the watch he wears! If I wear it, I can be as competent and suave as him.'

In *All Marketers are Liars (Who Tell Authentic Stories)*, Seth Godin says that while marketers 'lie' to customers, the right audiences are complicit. They want to be lied to, or they wouldn't buy the story. For the watch itself we pay $50, for the story we pay $5,000. This necessitates telling a story that resonates with what might be a very specific audience, and being willing to alienate the rest.

Incidentally, individual product stories are useful for price segmentation and product diversification. A client who is the head of marketing for a global enterprise recently told me about his work with a previous employer. When he started, their most expensive cigar was priced at $30. By the time he left, they were selling cigars for $500 each ... and which only cost $1 more to produce. The difference? Storytelling around brand identity and how the tobacco was aged for more than 10 years (which it was).

Remember my story about the United Nations agencies? Incidentally, that was an example of a *solution story* or *sales story*. A problem you can fix for clients. Instead of pitching someone directly – especially if they are not yet a client – you can tell a story about how you solved someone else's problem and allow the other person to come to their own conclusion about the fact that you could help them with their problem, too.

This is exactly what happened to me. A few weeks later, I was coaching the president of an NGO, and mentioned the UN agency story. It turned out this gentleman was having a similar problem: his employees were all quarrelling over their organisation's strategy, and during our conversation the president realised they would never reach unity as long as they were talking in the abstract. Towards the conclusion of our session, the gentleman paused and said: "We've been working with a strategy consultant, but hearing all this, I think I'd rather work with you." Sometimes the power of story catches even me by surprise. By sharing an anecdote, I'd unintentionally planted the idea in his head that storytelling might succeed where the traditional organisational approach had failed.

Model the Sale

There's nothing worse than a tired sales spiel. Sometimes salespeople just don't sound quite human. You can tell they're giving you a script – that sounds like it was written by a robot. The human alternative is to tell and listen out for stories, like I did with the aforementioned NGO president. Telling a sales story like that is remarkably simple with this framework: *Your client had a problem until they met a guide and made a plan that avoided failure and ended in success.* Let's unpack this.

1. **Your client**. Who was this other client? What did they want? You want the person you're talking with to identify with this character, so try and cast this other client in the role of the story's protagonist or hero. Don't even mention they were your client – yet. Just introduce us to them. This will ensure the story is powerful and authentic rather than an obvious sales pitch.

2. **Had a problem**. Why couldn't this client achieve their goal? What was their problem? Why was this terrible and how did it make them feel? This is where you rope in prospective clients. If they could not identify with the hero in the first sentences, e.g. because they are in a different industry, then they should now recognise: Hey, I have that same problem! Now they will be hooked, and you'll have their undivided attention.

3. **Until they met a guide**. How did the client meet you? Did someone recommend you to them? Did you help them in the past, or had they always wanted to work with you? These are all useful things to mention to cement your credibility.

4. **And made a plan**. Describe how you made the plan together with the client. Stories model behaviour. If you've succeeded in getting your prospect to identify with your other client, then the person you're talking with is now mentally picturing themselves making a plan with you. What were your client's objections about the plan? This is the place to address your *current* lead's assumed or admitted concerns.

5. **That avoided failure**. Did something (nearly) go wrong? How did you save the situation? What would have happened if you hadn't been there? Remind your prospect what was at stake and why it was so important to get your help. This is where you demonstrate additional competence and can further differentiate yourself from competitors.

6. **And ended in success**. What was the result? Externally – were they complimented by their boss or other stakeholders? What happened with the metrics? And internally – how did the client feel having resolved the problem and being able to celebrate success?

Remember: people buy for emotional reasons and justify the decision rationally later. So mention how your client felt in step 2, at the height of the problem. And then make sure they're feeling the opposite by step 6. This is the feeling your new prospect wants, which is why they are much more likely to work with you now, having heard your sales story.

Contrast this with the case study, which usually casts your organisation as the 'hero' and neglects the human element – the reason that people buy. If your salespeople talk in stories instead that feature real people with concrete problems and feelings, prospective clients are much more likely to engage. And, as we discussed earlier, prospective clients are much more likely to respond to a sales story with a story of their own. What does this mean here? They're acknowledging you as the guide (step 3). At which point you can jump to step 4 and start making a plan with them that addresses their particular pain, emphasise how this will help them avoid failure, and paint a picture of their future success.

EXERCISE

- Collect your most interesting success stories and put them into the six-part framework. File them away in your story bank under the hashtag #sales or #success. More on that in Part 3.

- Are you still trying to sell your product or service in terms of its production cost, or can you increase its perceived value with a story? Are you selling features or benefits? On your website and marketing collateral, do you talk about yourself as the hero, or can you demonstrate service from the start by casting yourself in the role of the guide who wants your customer to succeed on their own hero's journey?

6 – Destiny
Hack Yourself

The most important person to get buy-in with and have a strategy for is not your boss, your organisation or your customers – it's you. Besides, it wouldn't be fair if we hacked everyone else but not ourselves, would it? Agreeing to try and hack yourself means you're being honest as a storyteller, because you recognise that stories should be told in service of others. This is the section where we explore how you can tell stories *to yourself* to serve *you*.

Because we're all telling ourselves stories all the time. The question is: are yours serving you? Or are you, like most people, the unwitting victim of a bad story?

British psychology professor Richard Wiseman wanted to understand why some people seem to be luckier than others. Partnering with the BBC, he installed hidden cameras in a café and followed a man and a woman who respectively self-identified as very lucky or very unlucky. The experiment consisted of creating two 'chance' opportunities and seeing what happened.

The first opportunity was a crisp £5 note they placed on the pavement outside the café. The second was filling the café with actors so there was only one empty seat, which happened to be at a table occupied by a successful businessman.

What do you think happened?

The 'lucky person' found the £5 note, bought the business leader a coffee and struck up a conversation that might lead to further opportunities. The 'unlucky person' missed the money and sat in silence next to the business leader, nursing their coffee.

Why do you think this happened? People who self-identify as lucky are optimistic. And because they expect good things to happen, they keep an eye out for them. They are observant and quick to seize opportunities. People who consider themselves unlucky on the other hand are more likely to be dejected and inward-focused, so confronted with the same opportunities, they do not spot them. Further, the lucky person is more willing to be generous. He'd found the £5 anyway, why not buy the pleasant-looking bloke a coffee?

Attitude matters, and that depends on your story. Whether you think you can, or you think you can't – you're right. Our internally narrated stories tend to come true. "The stories we tell ourselves about our lives don't just shape our personalities – they *are* our personalities" writes Dan McAdams, psychology professor at Northwestern University in his book, *The Redemptive Self: Stories Americans Live By*.

Who am I and what do I want in life? What do I care about? Why do I do what I do? These are all very basic and important questions, and the interesting fact for our purposes is that they are all *story questions*.

The way you answer these questions will become part of your personal meta-narrative. You can think of this as your 'self-talk', though in reality your self-talk is likely to be informed by a deeper level still – subconscious narratives or 'scripts'.

Script is a pretty scary word, because it smacks of programming. And that's exactly what scripts do: they have us programmed. Personal meta-narratives are the bedrock from which your self-talk springs. This is why many people find changing their self-talk so hard: it is merely a symptom, not the root of the problem.

Edit Your Self-Narrative

Lori Gottlieb does not call herself a psychotherapist, though that is her profession. She introduces herself to strangers as an *editor*. By helping clients reframe the stories of their past, she changes their present and their future.

Change your story, change your world.

In her book, *Maybe You Should Talk to Someone*, Gottlieb writes: "Therapy is about understanding the self that you are. But part of getting to know yourself is to unknow yourself—to let go of the limiting stories you've told yourself about who you are so that you aren't trapped by them, so you can live your life and not the story you've been telling yourself about your life."

Limiting stories? Are these psychologists talking metaphorically instead of using industry jargon? No, they mean this quite literally. In fact, it's led to a whole new field of study: narrative psychology, which examines how stories shape our lives and personalities.

Our subconscious is a story generator. When we go to sleep, we tell ourselves stories. Dreaming is the process of making sense of everything that happens to us by bringing it into some kind of narrative shape. This makes stories your most powerful ally . . . or your unseen, worst enemy.

Sir Richard Branson was a rambunctious boy with dyslexia. When he dropped out of school at 16, it was to start, of all things, a magazine. Yes, Britain's most celebrated entrepreneur got his start as a dyslexic magazine editor. In *David and Goliath*, Malcolm Gladwell writes about how a disproportionate number of overachievers are dyslexic. Not because dyslexia has any inherent advantages – in fact it has many disadvantages – but because it is precisely those disadvantages that force dyslexics to compensate by bolstering other strengths. Of course, these people are the exception, and whether a dyslexic will adapt creatively or be beaten down depends on other factors.

We all see the world through the lens of the stories that have shaped us. To understand someone's opinions and behaviour, we must know the 'I' behind the 'eyes'. To change opinion and behaviour – even our own – we must engage the internal 'I', another person's or our own source beliefs, not merely the 'eyes', the attitudes and behaviours resulting from those beliefs.

We are the sum of our stories – the result of our own experiences, but also of second-hand experiences we have been told about. These experiences go into our subconscious as 'stories', informing our perception about the nature of reality, other people, and ourselves. Sometimes we remember the source, sometimes we don't. When we do, consciously reminding ourselves of that story can be a source of strength. A client of mine, CEO of a family business, had been impacted by a fantasy novel in his youth, especially by its theory of right and wrong. When he faces a tough personal decision, such as letting someone go, this CEO sees himself as Richard from Terry Goodkind's *Sword of Truth* series, wielding the sword with love rather than hate.

Flip the Script

We always have the option to reframe our story. When my income from book royalties dried up, I admit I was not keen to pursue business storytelling work. I liked the idea, but it left a bad taste – the feeling of just doing it for the money because I'd failed to survive (at least for the time being) as a full-time novelist. Also, building a new career couldn't be done overnight. For short-term security, I swallowed my pride and took on my first ever (part-time) day job. And because I wanted to keep writing novels, I spent the next year and a half juggling three jobs . . .

One of the most interesting moments in any story is the moment when the protagonist is forced to look herself in the mirror and do a reality check. That's what happened with me. Feeling overwhelmed and hopeless, I had to question my own internal narrative. Other people's true stories of struggle, unexpected connections and creativity were for me always tremendously inspiring and motivating, but it took a while for the penny to drop. Finally, while reading about a woman who designs living environments for people with special needs, I realized that the ability to convey this kind of inspiration and instruction was precisely what I loved about stories. A simple story could give someone something money couldn't buy: hope. For oneself. Or hope in humanity in general. And that could set them off on a whole new trajectory.

Becoming as passionate about business storytelling as I had been about fiction led to a boost in the numbers, too. After what had been only a trickle of opportunities, I now found myself booked out.

Because my earlier story had cast me in the role of a failed novelist and a victim of my circumstance, it sapped my energy and led to self-sabotage. When I realized I wasn't stuck in a bad story, it opened my perspective and opportunities. The attitude shift made me pitch differently, with more confidence, not second guessing myself.

The most persuasive storytellers *live* their story. Harvard psychologist Howard Gardner talks about how the best leaders embody their story. But there is the flip side of the coin: the best lives come from good stories.

Improve Quality of Life

If you have quality products or ideas, have patience and look for the authentic stories. You won't have to look far to find them. The beauty of storytelling is that it elevates the ordinary.

Thinking like a storyteller will generally improve your quality of life, because you start noticing the small things. The magical moments that otherwise pass us by in the rush to 'accomplish' things. Which brings us to the big things. Often, we're so focused on 'priorities' that we neglect *purpose*, from which priorities should flow.

Examining your dominant 'life story' as well as appreciating individual incidents helps you take back your time, because you take note of what happens rather than letting it all become one long, busy blur. You start getting insights into your own behaviour, which is right up at the peak of Maslow's pyramid (self-actualisation).

Another area not to be underestimated is personal authenticity. Do your stories align to certain core values, for instance integrity, honesty, respect, inclusion, doing the right thing etc.? And critically, is there alignment between the stories you tell yourself, and the stories you tell others? If not, at some level, you can't help but question whether you're for real.

Remember what we said in Part 1 about how the best stories make us feel more alive and want to be better people? By helping us reconnect to our own highest selves, stories can not only help us to gain others' trust. They can help us trust ourselves.

EXERCISE

- Reflect: How do you embody your story? Where is your internal narrative holding you back? Work at the questions consciously for a few minutes to allow the teeth of your subconscious to get a grip on them, and come back to this later.

- If you're not sure where to start, make sure you are not sabotaging yourself with a fixed mindset. Do you believe that when you fail, it is because you aren't smart enough? Or because of external circumstances? Or other people? If so you're making yourself into a victim. Take a minute to research the antidote: **growth mindset**. Rejecting the false narrative of a fixed mindset and adopting a growth mindset is probably the fastest way to improve your character and life.

- What is your definition of success? Is that really your own narrative or are you trying to live someone else's story?

There is obvious overlap between the six areas we've covered. Trust is a key component of buy-in. The six areas were just examples of how storytelling can revolutionise a particular key area. Merging the various areas can help you hack other specific areas. For example, if you can pique people's interest (hack 1), build trust (hack 2), and get people to agree with you (hack 3), you have everything you need to hack everything from major deals to job applications and interviews.

When people start understanding the incredible and diverse potential of storytelling to improve life and business, a lot of them get stressed. They really want to learn the skill, but they're worried they don't have the time or the creativity to master it. That's why our final section is on hacking stories.

Part 3:

How to Hack Stories

The most powerful person in the world is the storyteller.

- Steve Jobs

7 – Structure

Hack Stories

T alking about how to 'hack' stories is not without a certain irony, because in the arts, 'a hack' is someone deemed unoriginal and uninspiring. In our sense, hacking is about being efficient and effective . . . and, wonderfully, the process leaves us and our conversation partners feeling *more* human.

The Four Stages of Competence

I hope that reading about the first hack, conversations and meetings, built your confidence to talk simply and personally. If you're like most people, though, chances are you're still not confident about telling stories. In fact, at first your confidence may go *down*. That's a good sign! Why?

Because of the four stages of competence.

In any area that requires skill, we start in a position of *unconscious incompetence*: we don't know how bad we are at something.

It's an improvement when we realise just how little we know and how inadequate our existing skills are (*conscious incompetence*).

With knowledge and practice, we can eventually master *conscious competence*. We have the skills, but it costs effort.

Until we have practiced enough and finally arrive at *unconscious competence*.

When you've had some practice, you'll start seeing useful anecdotes everywhere, and sharing them will become second nature. But we can all use some help to get us started; and there are some things you don't want to leave to chance, such as how you talk about what you do professionally in a way that immediately attracts the interest of the right people.

Your 4 Ws

In my leadership coaching sessions, I help clients craft four key personal business stories that answer common questions people have – your '4Ws'. The thing to note is that while people have no qualms about asking, 'What do you do for a living?', most people may never pose the other three questions aloud:

1. Who are you? (Are you interesting?)
2. What do you do? (Are you relevant?)
3. Why are you here? (Are you trustworthy?)
4. Will your way work for me? (Can you solve my problem? Are you competent and can we work together?)

The four Ws are key personal business stories you can use on a daily basis – your who, your what, your why, and your way. Good responses to each can skyrocket your business. Given their importance and how often you need them, it's worth spending time on these four, gauging the response and periodically revisiting them. These oft-needed stories can also be the hardest to get right without outside help. By asking the right questions, a friend or coach can help you tap the rich narrative veins of your experience and hit story gold mines.

Your WHO answers the question: *Who are you?*

Function: Makes people more likely to work <u>with</u> <u>you</u> personally as they know/like/trust you more. Are you interesting and likeable?

Story prompt: What's unusual about you or your background? What experiences made you 'you'?

Personal example: *I was born in the UK to a British mother and Indian father and moved to Switzerland when I was seven … but I always wanted to live in another world: a world where there was more adventure, passion and purpose. That's what drew me to reading fiction, and soon reading wasn't enough. I started writing and published my first book at seventeen. I'm still passionate about fiction, but I've discovered how to help people discover these values in business too, which is why I'm in the field of business storytelling.*

As you can see, this kind of 'story' doesn't have to have happened all in one episode or place. It's all about making thematic connections.

Your WHAT answers the question: *What do you do?*

Function: Makes you relevant to the relevant people; models you solving their problems. Are you relevant to me or my contacts?

Story prompt: What value do you bring to the table from a customer's perspective?

For examples, see the sections *Increase Perceived Value* and *Model the Sale* in *5 – Desire: Hack Sales*. To start with, you can use the simple formula: *A lot of* [describe customers] *want* [describe desire], *but* [what they struggle with]. *After* x or *as* y [describe your experience/credentials], *I help* [achieve result]. Don't stress over whether or not this meets the criteria for a real story. It serves as excellent story bait – something to pique interest so you can follow up with an actual story, such as how you helped a particular customer with a concrete challenge (sales story).

Your WHY answers the question: *Why are you here? What's in it for you?*

Function: Builds more trust; goals that benefit you are okay as long as they are not exploitative.

Story prompt: What is important to you personally? Drives you? Excites you about your What?

Example of a surface-level why: my independent insurance broker described to me how he got a cut of deals he got me to sign up for, but explained how his commission did not result in higher expense for me, because if I bought a product directly at an insurer, their internal sales team would take that same commission. I was more than happy for him to get the commission rather than someone at a large insurance company. For a deeper level, see *Your Why* section in *2 – Empathy: Hack Trust*.

Your WAY answers the question: *(How) does it really work?*

Function: an experiential explanation, it removes barriers and makes people want to work with you.

Story prompt: What don't people see from the outset or the outside? What core parts of your process do clients have to understand to 'get it'? What differentiates your product or process? What do clients tend to appreciate that isn't clear to people until they become clients? Can you make it clear to people *before* they're clients (so they're more likely to end up as clients)?

For example, a client I've just written an image film for makes small kitchen appliances. Rather than just claiming they have 'the best' juicer or blender, they explain 'their way' to the results, such as getting more juice and wasting less food by means of a triangular container and geometric blades that perform up to 120,000 cuts per minute. If you can include something like 'most people in my industry do x,' and then contrast that with your way, so much the better. Again, this doesn't have to be an actual story in a strict sense. It could be an analogy, such as getting people to understand how you help them sharpen their axe.

In my line of work, I often talk about how stories let your stakeholders go beyond hearing an explanation of your product, to having an experience of it. I give the example of watching a scary movie and jumping when bad things happen, even though the rational part of your mind knows you're sitting on a sofa eating popcorn. What's scarier: the statement "being hunted is scary" or watching a character be hunted? The latter, of course.

That's because your subconscious thinks it's *in* the story. With this explanation, people immediately understand one key component of what makes storytelling work. What are the key components people have to understand about what you do?

A useful way to think of your 4Ws are as 'origin stories'. Why do you do what you do? How did it all start? Superheroes have origin stories. Even though we only spend the first episode of a comic or the first few minutes of a film exploring the character's past, without it, audiences don't usually care much about the hero. Well, if you have a 'superpower' (or super-passion) then it deserves an origin story too.

Acquiring Competence

It is very useful to have stories ready to answer these unspoken questions. It is even more useful to have the practice and the confidence to deliver them well. But where can you test these stories to make sure they work? And how can we get practice and be sure we're doing it well enough to use them in high-stakes business settings? How do you start?

This brings us full circle to our first hack. You do what you have to do anyway – you have conversations.

Oral storytelling is a skill you must hone. Because 'how are you' is a question always asked, it gives you a low-stakes, everyday opportunity to practice storytelling before you start using stories in more high-stakes settings.

Stories come so naturally to us, your counterparts often won't even realise you're pitching until you've piqued their interest. And by then it will be too late: if you've established an empathetic connection (Your Who story), they like you and *want* to trust you. They want to know more. The stage is set for your next story (e.g. Your Why).

Preparing story-form answers to the most common conversational topics forms your conversational capital. Investing the time to prepare stories can pay off every single day as it leads straight to social capital.

But what if they *don't* like your story? Well, if you're telling the right story and telling it well, chances are that the people who don't like it aren't the kind of customer you're looking for. If they're not qualified leads, be grateful. That person has done you both a favour by not wasting your time. Go and talk to someone who responds.

Two caveats:

- First, you must listen yourself. That's how you know which story to tell.
- Having the right story ready requires a collection.

Keep a Story Bank

If you want easy access to your capital, but don't want to lug it all around with you, where do you put it? In a bank. I recommend you do the same for your stories. Write them down and keep them somewhere safe and easily accessible, i.e. on your favourite note-taking app or in a notebook.

Spaced optimally, three retellings of a story will secure it in your long-term memory. You'll still want to write them down. There are seasons when you will need some stories more than others, and recording a story is the first opportunity to save its existence in your mind. If you're looking for just the right story for a speech, having your stories in front of you will help you pick the right ones. There are also times when you just jot down a story fragment. Maybe it's not complete because you haven't had time to write down the whole story. Maybe there was a hint of a story in the newspaper you want to research later. Maybe you experience something that might yet become a great story. In these cases, you could use a tag such as 'fragment', to which you can return later.

Organise your stories according to what makes sense to you, but I *do* recommend ordering them. So you might choose headings such as 'mindset', 'humour', and, for stories you yourself experienced, 'me'. Apps that use tags such as Evernote or Google Keep are perfect, because if you're like me, you won't be satisfied with one way of ordering them, you'll want something more dynamic; the same story is likely to be labelled both 'me' and 'leadership' and perhaps 'culture' or 'travel' if it was something I experienced in another country.

Obviously, four important stories to secure in your story vaults are your 4Ws. But coming up with them can be hard. In fact, the number one storytelling problem my clients have is finding useful personal stories. At best, they end up with a string of incidents. But no sense of completion. No insight. Nothing worthy of a story. They stare at the blank page, growing increasingly stressed about the fact they aren't coming up with anything. That's what writers deal with all the time. But you don't need to suffer from writer's block. You already have a wealth of experiences that could make for powerful stories. All you have to do is assemble your stories block by block.

Farm for Fragments

It's much easier to collect stories than to craft them – which is why your story bank is so important. Without a story collection, you might struggle to develop or remember one on the spot, which can be dangerous. Your mind is working and you aren't fully listening to your counterpart. Chances are your story will meander and be without decipherable meaning. Instead of coming up with stories *on the spot*, it's much better to *spot* stories, collect, and spotlight them.

Often, you'll be in the middle of a conversation with someone and before you know it, you've told them a story. A pretty good one. As soon as possible, excuse yourself and secure it in your story bank. Save time by leaving yourself a voice memo. There's nothing worse than mistyping a thought, going back to correct your spelling or wording, and realising you've forgotten what you were going to write next. So you'll probably want to voice record or dictate even if you're alone.

If you are in conversation and the situation allows, why not even beg their indulgence and explain you're developing a story bank, so would they mind holding that thought while you record a few sentences? If your counterpart is interested in the topic, it could be an opportunity to test a story or two.

When you're looking out for them, spotting stories is easy. You or someone else tells a good one, you write it down and file it away. But what about developing your own stories? You need to spot those too. They're just harder to spot, because they're usually incomplete, and we don't have them somewhere we can see them.

Remember how in our definition of story we talked about the importance of moments? Thinking of stories as *thematically connected moments* makes our job so much easier. It's a lot easier to remember a moment than a complete story. But that's all a story is: moments that have been meaningfully connected. So that's where we need to start – by coming up with a list of moments. Grab a large piece of paper or open an app and list all the memories you can. Are these moments isolated and maybe meaningless? That's okay. We'll connect the dots later. For now, just collect as many of them as possible. I call these incidents **story fragments**. They are the individual links from which we will craft an unbreakable chain of events – a compelling story.

Now you've got these memories down, start exploring the connections. Just the fact you're writing these memories down will start prodding your subconscious to come up with more. And because we think associatively, chances are that as you record your stream of consciousness, your mind will throw out story fragments that belong together. All you need is two or three - and voila! There's your story!

Story fragments usually lack meaning because they are alone. Just like humans. We draw our meaning from relationships. Stories are, above all, *relational*. They are about relationships between people and people, or people and issues – and how those relationships changed. So when looking for stories, it can help to look relationally. Think of story fragments as orphans looking to be adopted. As soon as you have two fragments, they are in relation to one another, and have the stuff of meaning.

Connect the Dots

Let me give you an example from my own life. I was recently walking in the vineyards that give my city its name (Weinfelden), and was enjoying the beautiful scenery. It was hazy, and the mountains were just a silhouette. *Too bad*, I thought. *I love it when the mountains are clear*. Suddenly, I remembered a family trip to the mountains as a teenager. After a two-hour drive, we reached some steep, windy roads. Which annoyed me, because I just wanted to read my book. I looked outside the window and glared at the mountains. "Oh, wow. Mountains. Great," I said sarcastically. "I know they're supposed to be beautiful and stuff, but so what? I don't get it. It just doesn't do anything for me."

That's a story fragment. An unspectacular, isolated incident.

I continued my walk through the vineyards, smiling wistfully at the memory. I grew melancholy, because my mother always had to drag us on family outings like that. I must have been insufferable company. What a little brat I was! I started to regret my ungrateful behaviour. For a long time now, I have absolutely adored beautiful scenery. *When did the change happen?*

My next thought was my subconscious answering that question. When I was about fourteen, I got my first pair of spectacles. I vaguely remembered the teacher telling me off for not being able to read the blackboard, and thinking I was messing with her. "If you're really struggling to read my writing, go and get your eyes checked." Which I eventually did, only to discover I was short-sighted. I remembered getting my first pair of spectacles, and how the world looked like a new place. How clean and clear everything looked when it was in focus – *washed* somehow.

Another story fragment.

Not just any fragment. The missing piece. As soon as it came to me, I knew I had a story. Part one (setup), and part two (resolution). Complaining that outings to the mountains were a waste of time. Complaining about people going all the way there to see the beauty, when who cares about beauty? *Because I literally couldn't see it.* But that revelation would come from part two, the scene about the blackboard, and how getting spectacles made me fall in love with the beauty of nature again.

It was an incredibly rewarding walk. I hadn't just enjoyed nature. By reflecting on my changing relationship towards natural beauty, I had reconnected with my earlier self. Needless to say, as soon as I got home, I opened my story bank and stored the new nugget.

Collecting stories can either be an occasional chore or an enjoyable habit. I encourage you to develop the latter. Think of the process as being more like farming than hunting. It's hard to decide what kind of story you need and try and force your brain to hunt it down. The subconscious is like farmland. Sow some seeds and see what grows. Keep coming back and adding to your paper. Explore the relationships between your story fragments. Ask questions and let them percolate in the back of your mind.

There is an exception to the 'farming' approach. Obviously if you need a specific story and don't have time to farm your fragments, you do need to hunt that story down. A story coach can ask you the right questions to guide your subconscious to the memories you need, and help make connections between seemingly random life incidents, so you can turn cute memories into compelling stories.

The 1-2-1 Story Formula

A few years ago, my friend Kevin Brinkmann was excited to teach storytelling to a group of blind social entrepreneurs in India. Kevin has trained people at organisations like Canon, PWC and the World Bank, but he knew he needed something simple and above all *usable* for these rural innovators. So he came up with the 1-2-1 story formula, the simplest way of telling a story. While I have formulas of my own, they are specific to the context in which you are telling your story. So with credit to Kevin, I'm giving you his here, because it's a great hack to get you started.

What are the biggest challenges people have to overcome in business storytelling?

- Stories are irrelevant
- They're boring
- People forget them

The 1-2-1 story formula solves these three problems:

- **1 point** ensures the story is relevant.
- **2 halves** makes it interesting.
- **1 unforgettable detail** makes it memorable.

One point: In business, when you have to cut to the chase, it's a good idea to start by telegraphing your point. "I learned an important lesson about [topic related to the issue at hand] when [time and location]." Now build your story around making that one point and don't meander. It might last between thirty and ninety seconds, unless you're performing onstage and are expected to entertain an audience. Make sure the point serves your audience, so they'll want to listen.

Two halves: While you don't want to meander, you do want to create a sense of progress – of change. This is most easily achieved by dividing a story into *before* and *after*. The first half is the setup; the second half is the payoff. Or it may follow the structure of problem–solution, or of expectation-surprise. Often, there is a watershed moment of realisation or transformation. If you tried a new approach, that approach might be the point of your story.

1 unforgettable detail: Specifics make stories come alive. In a one-minute business story, it's enough to have just one striking detail that will paint a picture in the mind. It could be an image, such as when the chairman of the company got down on hands and knees to help a junior clerk finish a display. Or it could be a powerful line of

dialogue. This unforgettable detail can – but does not have to – encapsulate the point of the story. It could just be description that engages the brain's sensory or motor cortex.

Example: When RockTenn CEO Worley Brown was faced with a plant that was losing millions of dollars, people expected him to fire everyone and shut down the plant. Instead, he met with each and every shift worker to tell them: "I believe in you. What is it that you need?" One year later, these same people had turned their plant into the company's most productive.

One point: Believe in your people, and they will perform (the Pygmalion Effect).

Two halves: Before, the plant was losing millions. After, it was the best performing.

Unforgettable detail: "I believe in you. What do you need?"

One reason I like Kevin's story formula is because it corresponds with the way I approach all storytelling, no matter the formula. First, I look for the **substance**. What point do you want to make and what incident(s) will prove that point? Second, the incident needs to be narrated with a **structure** so that it is an experience rather than information (and so that it fits your audience, occasion and medium). Finally, bring your own unique **style** to the podium. So don't feel like you need to copy me, or Steve Jobs, or anyone else. What worked for someone else may not work for you. Learn from everyone, try out everything, but only keep what works for you.

EXERCISE

- Draw three columns for the 1-2-1 story formula and use each to brainstorm points you want stories to make, what the two halves look like (setup and payoff), and a corresponding unforgettable detail.

- Look to your story bank and story fragments for inspiration. For example, you may realise that one of your 'orphan' fragments is actually the second half for a story. Different methods work for different brains at different times, so keep switching back and forth and coming back to these exercises. Connections *will* spark.

Banking on Stories

What a story bank can do for you personally, it can also do for your organisation. A collective story repository quickly becomes a powerful resource for everyone from new recruits to the CEO. When you recruit, it will dramatically save time. New executives who've joined your company will gain an understanding of how your organisation does business, what your clients expect, how your organisation approaches communications, sales, and so on – all at the same time. When your representatives meet with the government, regulators, partners or suppliers, a story bank will help them go beyond an 'update' and help stakeholders receive, believe and remember your message. It's also a great way of building investor relations.

When a team or the board meets, a story bank helps you go beyond the abstract and give people a common vocabulary and concrete images to work with. When you need to give clarity with a big-picture x story, open the story bank and find small stories that illustrate the steps of your larger narrative. When people hit decision paralysis, they can quickly consult the organisation's values *in action*, which will often model the solution.

Before making an endless list of tags, you'll want to think about the workflow. Start by listing the various departments that could use the story bank according to their function and corresponding need (executives, sales, marketing, HR, engineers, etc.). Who needs to be consulted and who would need to roll this out? Do you already use software that is up to the task, or do you need to research whether to use Evernote, Google Keep, Notion, or whatever other notetaking app is best by the time you read this?

What about entries and access? Can everyone pool entries? Do stories need to be edited and approved? Who maintains the organisation's story bank? Should there be sections that can only be accessed by certain departments for some reason? By nature, stories are viral, so restricting access is the exception – and in such cases it may be better simply to use a separate 'eyes only' story bank.

Opt for a test phase for the organisational story bank. Can you pioneer it informally among a handful of colleagues before approaching the person whose buy-in you need to roll it out? If you're at a large organisation, include a few people from different departments.

But try and keep it simple. All you may need is what you use for your own personal story bank. That said, giving it some thought can help you set it up so it's actually useful to as many people as possible, because it will save an enormous amount of time for your fellow executives and employees.

Strategy is supposed to guide behaviour explicitly, but rarely does, unless it's been storified. Culture is the implicit guide to behaviour. Change the stories, change the culture. Stories model behaviour. When stories are managing people and guiding their behaviour, you don't need to. An organisational story bank is its very own hack for knowledge management . . . and for management, full stop.

EXERCISE

- Create a list of your hashtags (functions, topics, emotions, industry, geography etc.). For each word, try and remember a story or two. Don't expect your subconscious to find these immediately. This is hard for most of us because so far, our subconscious didn't think remembering stories was important. Keep coming back to this list. It will get easier each time.

- Next, float the idea of an organisational story bank. Sell the idea with a story: give an example of how your personal story bank has helped you.

Resolution

Back from the Hack

T his guide was my attempt to hack the task of teaching storytelling. We've covered a lot of ground in a short space. I hope it has been insightful and instructional to you.

When I take on a new coaching client, I usually spend several sessions covering the basics. With this guide, people can grasp the basics and come to me for help with application and with fine-tuning. That's better value for clients and more fun for me.

Now it's my turn to ask you for a favour. I'm eager to keep learning and improving, and serving my clients better. So I would appreciate your feedback. Please leave a **review** containing everything positive you can possibly say – especially how the book has helped you achieve your objectives – at your favourite platforms such as Amazon and Goodreads. But do send all negative comments, complaints, disagreements, questions and constructive criticism to me (jyoti@guptara.com).

To fit with the idea of a hack, I had to keep this book short, which forced me to leave a lot out. What would you like to learn more about? What do I need to fix? What do we really need to take apart in more detail? Or can you share a story about success you've had with storytelling?

Such comments are valuable to me. You see, I'm working on a much longer, comprehensive book on business storytelling . . . but that's another story. Feel free to subscribe to my author letter to stay informed of future publications. You'll hear from me only a few times a year.

Finally, there is **another** reason I chose to publish this guide in this way at this time. You might like to hear it if only as another example of personal storytelling.

In January 2019, after a brave battle with cancer, my mother died two weeks before her 70th birthday. I arrived just a few hours too late to say goodbye in person. Wanting to do something in her memory, my father founded a publisher with her (maiden) name, Pippa Rann.

It is my delight to publish this guide with Pippa Rann Books & Media of Salt Desert Media Group, and I have enjoyed working with my father to publish and promote it. If you are interested in India, especially in light of democratic and humane values, perhaps he has published your next read (www.pipparannbooks.com).

Yours for messages that click and stick, and stories that move people.

— Jyoti

Jyoti Guptara, Switzerland, September 2020

About the Author

When Jyoti Guptara dropped out of school at the age of 15 to become a full-time writer, teachers couldn't imagine they'd be inviting him back three years later to speak as a bestselling author.

Writing together with his twin brother, Jyoti published a fantasy trilogy that sold over 100,000 copies in four languages. *Schweizer Illustrierte* magazine counted him among the '100 Most Important Swiss' and the County of Los Angeles awarded him a Scroll of Honour for Special Services to the County for philanthropy, literary achievement, and inspiring other young people.

Jyoti Guptara, despite being a successful novelist, did not appreciate the value of storytelling in business until he was a Fellow and Writer-in-Residence at a United Nations partner organisation. There, he realised that some of the best content came after and between presentations, informally – when people told stories. Guptara was initially invited to apply his decade of experience with fiction to executive education, helping business leaders find and tell stories to give better talks, pitch ideas and influence meetings – leading to his current work. Of British and Indian descent, Jyoti lives in Switzerland and consults internationally. He has spoken on four continents. www.guptara.com

Made in the USA
Columbia, SC
18 February 2023